Going for God

Going for God

The Story of Bessie Brierley

BETTY MACINDOE

HODDER AND STOUGHTON
LONDON SYDNEY AUCKLAND TORONTO

This book is dedicated to Miss Theresa Keogh to whom Mrs. Brierley wrote:

"There you are, framed and hung on the wall in the sitting-room in Bissau, just as in former days. Many of the new friends ask, 'Who is this senhora?' And I reply, 'She is the one who has prayed and sacrificed more than any other so that you in Portuguese Guinea might have the Gospel.'"

15.8.45.

Foreword

I don't know if it is the best moment to write a foreword when I have just finished reading the manuscript of this book. I have been thrilled to my depths, not only by the plain impact of this story of Bessie's life, but by the upsurge of joy which I find at this modern-day illustration of what the Lord said was the one essential for missionary-apostleship—the Holy Spirit in the earthen vessel. As C. T. Studd, the founder of the Worldwide Evangelization Crusade, said in his own inimitable way, "All God wants is a heart, and any old turnip will do for a head! As long as we are empty all is well, for then He fills with the Holy Ghost." And sometimes His servants are women, not men—Mary Slessor, Gladys Aylward, Bessie Brierley. Sacrifice and faith are still the true crusading standards, only now, thank God, the day has come when the ranks of missionary crusaders are being swelled by Africans, Asians and Latin Americans.

You will see what I mean as you read the story. It is an eye-opener to me to read of the raw conditions of Bessie's home-life. I first met her at Arthur's Mission in the East End of London. I noticed the rapt attention of this young woman in the small group which gathered nightly. But when she came straight up to me and asked if there was any chance that a girl like her could be a missionary. I thank God that I gave her the right answer. I told her that it is not a good education that makes a missionary, but the Holy Ghost. She was to face me up with that effectively enough some years later when, as you will read, the crisis moment came about her going alone into Portuguese Guinea. I cabled to her saying that she should come home and that the passage money would be provided. She thanked me for my concern, but added that it was not me who had sent her out but God. "The Holy Spirit tells me to go forward," she wrote. "He can save by many or by few. I go forward even though everybody says I am crazy to do so." It was then that the motto came into being among us, "The woman is the man to do the job!"

I have known and loved Bessie since those beginning days—just the human Bessie that Betty Macindoe now makes alive to us in these pages. If God can do as He has with Bessie, He can surely do something with all of us.

I feel I must add a word of thankfulness for what this story brings out so clearly too—that God also commissions the hidden ones, the people behind the scenes. We are grateful for those who participated with Bessie by continual sacrifices and persistent prayer and faith all through the years—her co-crusaders in Arthur's Mission, Miss Cowley, the Keoghs and the others.

She that "goeth forth and weepeth, bearing precious seed, shall doubtless come again with rejoicing, bringing her sheaves with her."

Norman Grubb
Former British Secretary of
the Worldwide Evangelization
Crusade.

I

WHAT WAS SHE doing in the Borough Market at this late hour, this fair-haired, blue-eyed scrap of humanity? In her own Cockney idiom, she was furaging—looking for damaged vegetables at give-away prices when the day's custom was over, or for some scrag ends of meat with which to flavour the family stewpot. Determination sent her round the stalls, bargaining with their owners till her straw basket could hold no more. Furaging was Bessie's speciality when school gave her her freedom. Even Smithfield Market and Covent Garden were within her range. Her older sister, Florence, preferred to busy herself with the household chores, helped by young Winnie when she could be dragged from her dolls and her games on the flat roof of their tenement home. There were the two little brothers, John and Norman, to be cared for, quite a handful when Mother was out at work in a fish-shop.

World War I and the cruelties of a hard-drinking, seafaring husband and father had brought the family to poverty and to living in overcrowded conditions in the squalid east end of London. With only two rooms at their disposal, the girls of the family shared a bed in one of them, while the others had to squeeze into the living-room along with the white-scrubbed table and the copper in the corner where the clothes were boiled on washdays.

But this was life. Somehow one learned to accept its hardships and enjoy its little pleasures. In its soil Bessie grew tough and disciplined, gentle and generous, brave and appreciative. On a fine Saturday afternoon she would take Winnie and the boys for a penny tramride to Greenwich Park. Their picnic would be scant bread-and-jam sandwiches and a bottle of water. Bessie hated the tramrides for they made her positively sick, but when money was sufficient, she endured them for the pleasure they gave to the others. Often enough the five-mile distance was covered on foot for, in those days, time seemed limitless and bare feet saved shoe-leather.

Occasionally there were lively, home-variety concerts when the neighbours' children would crowd into the living-room to watch and gape starry-eyed while Bessie, draped in a piece of curtaining and decorated with her mother's trinkets, acted, sang and recited. Florence would disappear into the bedroom to 'put on the gramophone'. No one was allowed to see it, and when there had to be a change of record, Bessie would go into the bedroom. Behind the tightly closed door the game of pretend carried on. The two girls took turns in singing the popular songs into the wide mouth of a large enamel jug. The effect was both stunning and convincing!

Uncle Bill, a bachelor of rather mean disposition who lived one flat down, became the butt of many of the children's practical jokes. Bessie would knock at his door with some urgency and call out with well-concealed impishness,

"Uncle Bill, come quickly! You should see our Win. She's gone all pale. She looks awful. You'll have to come, Uncle Bill."

Then she would dash upstairs again followed by a breathless Uncle Bill hurrying to the emergency. There, propped up in bed, would be Winnie, her face smothered in flour and the other youngsters grouped around her, wringing their hands in simulated anguish. Or Florence would call through Bill's open doorway, "Cup of tea in the pot, Uncle Bill, if you'd like one."

When he had made it to the upstairs flat, the 'tea' which Bessie poured out ceremoniously would be cold, slightly-coloured water.

The family grew up in the disciplines of poverty, insensitive to a degree to want and scarcity. Wood had to be fetched from a nearby sawmill to stoke the copper-fire. The shopping list which Mother would leave on the table for the girls to fetch after school would read something like this:

> ½ pint of milk
> 1d packet of tea
> 2d mixed jam in a cup.

Careful and managing housewife that she was, she always contrived to make warm and nourishing meals out of the very little they could afford. When the girls needed petticoats, she washed and bleached sugar-sacks, cut them to size and sewed them by hand. Their school uniforms were others' hand-downs, a plaid skirt and a long-sleeved blouse for each of the girls. Every night before going to bed they would wash through the soiled sleeves ready for wear next day. Whenever possible Bessie would run errands for neighbours and so make a few pennies, but payment from one particular woman was the use of her big wooden clothes mangle for the heavy household laundry.

From earliest days Bessie had a very strong affection for her mother, a woman of some refinement and strength of character. The daughter of prosperous parents, she had been trained in some of the finer arts, was a pianist of no mean ability and possessed outstanding singing talent. The family business, however, had failed when its finances were used to salvage two prodigal sons, and Bessie's mother, desperately in need of help and friendship, married the man who became a drag on her and a responsibility. Work was hard to come by, and long periods of unemployment brought distress and privation. In and out of employment of various sorts, Bessie's father finally took to sea as a ship's cook. For months on end he would be away from

home and, in some measure, the family benefited from his absences, for his return brought fresh misery with his drinking
and gambling habits. Tensions, word-battles, accusations and
blows were all too common. At one point the parents separated
and Bessie was sent away to live with an aunt. The family
moved home on several occasions, always in the slum area of
the city, always trying to make ends meet. Eventually they
settled in their seventh-storey flat in the high, square, drab
tenement building near to London Bridge and the Borough
Market.

This was the childhood home that held Bessie's deepest
memories. Coming in from school one afternoon, she saw the
hem of her mother's long, sack-cloth apron catch alight from
the wood protruding from the copper-fire and burst into flames.
In a second she was with her, forcing her to the ground. Then,
rolling her in the rag-rug which lay in front of the kitchen
range, she smothered the flames.

It was in this home that Bessie passed from girlhood to adolescence and her school days merged into work days. Education
was an ill-afforded luxury, not for the working-class of the
'twenties', so the two oldest girls left school as soon as they
were fourteen years of age. An aunt, who was a housekeeper
to a drapery establishment, took them under her charge
and they became resident waitresses with the firm. This
relieved the home situation financially and accommodation-
wise, for the two boys and Winnie were fast growing up.
Later the two girls took their separate ways, Bessie finding
employment as a waitress in a restaurant in the Borough High
Street.

But before all this, before work took her away from home,
something happened to Bessie which was to be the beginning of
a new way of life for her. She loved to go to Sunday School for
it gave her somewhere to go and something to do on a Sunday
afternoon. And she loved singing. She was on her way through
the Park one Sunday afternoon when a friend called after her,

"Say Bess, why don't you come to *our* place? You'd get better treats there."

The thought was appealing. It caused her to turn in the direction of Arthur's Mission, Bermondsey, one of the Shaftesbury Mission Halls which had a special concern for the children from deprived homes. Rough and shabby the youngsters were who attended, but there at Arthur's, appearances did not matter much. Loving and caring were the priorities. There certainly were the 'treats' of food, clothing, outings, parties, but also regular instruction from the Bible. Bessie was no different from the others. She would swear, pilfer and indulge in fisticuffs. Then she would wish she could stop, for her conscience was being awakened to a sense of right and wrong.

After four years of regular attendance at Arthur's Mission she had a ready answer when her teacher, at the end of class, asked her if she would like to give herself to the Lord Jesus Christ. She could not have explained then in theological terms what happened as she knelt by a chair in one of the smaller rooms of the Mission, her teacher beside her, and prayed for forgiveness and acceptance. There could hardly have been a plainer spot or a simpler ceremony, scarcely noticed in that great city, but recorded in heaven. None could have imagined then that, from this act of committal, a life was to grow and develop and extend through training and experience to reach beyond the confines of a city's slums to another nation and continent and eventually to compass the world in its influence.

2

THE BIBLE CLASS girls were seated round the dining-room table in Miss Tubb's flat. She was their leader and this was their customary mid-week instruction hour. Her concern was to point them to the way of personal surrender to the Lord Jesus Christ leading them to a life of fullness and holiness. Bessie confessed that she did not understand all that was being shared, but she did know that God was probing into her soul, asking her if she was willing to make a full committal. There and then she made her reply—that life for her was no longer to be self-pleasing but obedience to Him. On the way home with the others she asked them to wait for a bit till she explained to them what had happened and what her intentions were, how she was determined never to be the same person with all her selfishness but to live only for Jesus Christ.

Some Sundays later she attended service in a nearby church where a visiting American preacher illustrated his theme by a story that struck her sensitive heart. She was so stirred that she felt compelled to go home at once and tell her family how greatly they needed to believe the Gospel and be saved. But having made the decision, she found it not so easy to carry out. By the time she opened the door to her home, her nerves were having a game with her. She put off talking to her family till they were all at their meal. When she started to speak, her eyes filled with tears. However, she went on to discharge her responsibility, although to her dismay not one of them responded at that time. She felt utterly defeated but never lost faith for them.

That act of obedience opened up the way for God to make His intentions further known to her in a call to the mission-field. Mr. Norman Grubb, then General Secretary of the World-wide Evangelization Crusade, had a series of talks at Arthur's Mission when the focus was on the unreached parts of the world. Then too the ministry of Mrs. Edith Moules, a missionary from Congo whom God had set apart for leprosy work, greatly impressed her. Just as clearly as on previous occasions, God's voice came through the Bible: "As you have testified at Jerusalem, so you must also testify at Rome."

She knew what God meant in her own circumstances for she had already witnessed to her family, her friends and those who shared the same corner of London's slumland. Now she must go much further and tell others in another land. Who can explain the quiet urging of the Spirit of God, but when He comes with urgent insistence, who can doubt or resist His promptings? So Bessie looked at the situation and thought how ridiculous a proposition it all was—that God should ever want *her*, poor, uneducated Bessie Fricker for the mission-field. That took a bit of believing from her own point of view. And how was she ever to tell anyone else?

She thought of Miss Cowley at the Mission, a school-teacher with her own private school for girls. What would she say? But Miss Cowley did not laugh at her. A godly woman, she recognised in Bessie the qualities for which God was looking, and with encouraging assurance she told her that she always knew that God would do something special with her life. Then to give reality to her thoughts, she took Bessie on as a pupil in English grammar after her day's work was over.

She thought of her widowed mother in need of every penny that the girls brought into the home. How could she ever tell her mother? And how could she ever leave her? For three days she prayed over what she should say and how to say it. When finally she could hold back no longer, she spilled out her intentions to her mother only to be surprised by the reply, "Well, your sister Win chose to get married and I did not stand in her way. Why should I stand in yours if you choose another life?" Her heart was relieved and released. She could sing again.

She thought of her manageress at the restaurant. She would have to explain why she was giving her a month's notice. She broached the subject with caution, waiting for the reaction. It was humiliating.

"Bessie, when you are gone I shall send your poor mother some groceries from time to time."

Bessie listened with hurt pride, and with her heart at breaking-point she hurried out of the shop and sobbed all the way home. Yet, for the glory of God, it must be said that from the time that Bessie left her wage-earning employment to follow her call, she never failed to send some small allowance regularly to her mother all the years of her long life.

She thought of her best friends, the Keogh family. Mr. and Mrs. Keogh, father and mother to seven children of their own, found a place in their home and their affections for yet another. When her father came back from his sea voyages, Bessie would take refuge from his tongue and his beatings in the comfort of the Keogh family circle. The children became veritable brothers and sisters to her, and over the years, as the circle was enlarged through marriages, the intimate relationships remained. To them the call of God to Bessie was a joy to be shared, a responsibility to be undertaken with all gladness and genuine affection. Theresa Keogh was Bessie's closest friend, and although they knew that there would be hurt in separation, their friendship was sealed in the fellowship of unremitting prayer, a friendship and fellowship which kept them in contact by letters throughout Bessie's years of service and miles of travel. Bessie wrote to Theresa from every new address, from every new location, and almost always in her own handwriting. These personal letters numbering hundreds, carefully kept, have formed an invaluable basis for much of this biography. There was also a deeper friendship with one of the boys of the family, but now with the call of God becoming very clear and His purposes for the future lying beyond the confines of Bermondsey, there came the moment of handing back the ring. It took a brave heart and a dogged determination to do so, and for days afterwards her emotions were in turmoil.

When the news of Bessie's call filtered through to the members of Arthur's Mission, they responded magnificently. A fund was opened for 'Our Own Missionary' and before Bessie left London for the Bible College of Wales, there to do her three years' missionary training, the Mission friends had bought her a dress, a coat and a watch. Above all, she was going assured of their prayers and practical support. Some girls worked overtime to give extra money towards Bessie's fees.

The moment for her to leave had come. At Victoria Coach Station, an excited, chattering group gathered to wave her off. Perhaps not quite knowing what was appropriate on such occasions one of the number started off the song, 'For she's a jolly good fellow', as the coach pulled out taking Bessie away to the autumn term's studies of 1932.

It was a glorious ride out of the city and into the country lanes of Berkshire and Wiltshire and on into South Wales. But tears kept welling up till Bessie was ashamed of her red eyes and of the glances from the gentleman opposite. At last she composed herself and thought of what lay ahead. Why, to be in Bible College and to be able to study the Bible for three whole years—that must be heaven upon earth! So she began to anticipate . . .

3

BESSIE'S FIRST DAY at the Bible College of Wales was a shattering experience. She had left school at fourteen years of age and now she was twenty-three. During the intervening years work had been a household necessity and Bessie had been both capable and enthusiastic. In her service in the Mission too she had proved her devotion and her untiring willingness. But serious study had never been part of her programme, so that to be seated in front of a blackboard—'the blackest I have ever seen'—on which was outlined an intelligence assessment test, was not quite what she had expected at Bible College!

She tackled the arithmetical problems with some measure of understanding, but when it came to questions on English grammar she was at a loss. She had a vague idea about a verb and a noun, but not a clue as to what a preposition looked like! When at last she handed in her paper she was sure that her failure was so complete that she would be turned out. Hopeless discouragement chased sleep away from her that night, and first thing in the morning she apologetically presented herself at the tutor's study door, hoping that by getting a word in first she could blunt the edge of his wrath.

"Sir," she blurted out quickly before he had had time to do more than recognise her, "I'm afraid I made an awful mess of my paper yesterday. But I *know* that God has called me to the

18

mission field." She waited and watched while a smile of friendly understanding crossed his face.

"Yes," he replied, "*I* know that God has called you."

From then on he spared no effort so that Bessie's standard of education should be improved. And while he placed his fund of knowledge and experience at her disposal, she was impressed by his gentlemanly humility, his graciousness and the measure of his sacrifice. With his Cambridge degree, he could have been living comfortably, but his choice left him in such poverty that at night his one shirt would be drying over the radiator ready for next day's wear.

Study did not come easily to Bessie. The variety of subjects included in the course baffled her. "Such a lot of stuff they make you learn at Bible College," she used to say. "Far above my poor brains. Psychology and ethics . . . I hardly understand a word. Imagine trying to make a psychologist out of me!"

Often she bemoaned her own dullness and frequently wrote of her dread of examinations. She tried in every way to do well, snatching odd moments of her recreation time to study her Greek declensions, producing from her uniform sleeve scraps of paper on which were scribbled memo notes so that she could glance at them between classes, tucking herself up with her study book in the only available warmth of bed on a Saturday afternoon while others were enjoying their well-earned break.

"That first year was as hard as could be. Those first examinations were pretty well a failure even after I had burned the midnight oil and plodded determinedly to get somewhere. Knowledge just doesn't fall from the skies," she later testified. But her determination did get her somewhere—sometimes to the very top of the examination list and often her name appeared amongst the first three.

"Examinations started Wednesday and went on till this morning. We sat for five subjects; you can't imagine how much we had to do . . . I praise the Lord for bringing me through. I didn't dream I would get on so well. It really is encouraging to get some good marks. I've been up all the week at 4.45 a.m. and not turned into bed till much before midnight . . . I did my best and He made me a *sticker*!"

If study was obligatory routine at College, prayer was priority with faith coupled to it. The students' example was no less a person than Mr. Rees Howells, Founder and Principal of the College. Bessie wrote, "He is a man full of faith and the Holy Spirit. His great theme is to *live* the word of God before preaching it. This week he has been taking us through Daniel, and it has been great. He is praying for £10,000 to build a school for missionaries' children, a rest home for missionaries and accommodation for a hundred students. What faith! He is *sure* God is going to do it too!"

Prayer for the everyday situations, faith for the practical details—this was a new way of life for Bessie, but her whole being responded to it as it became her personal decision to walk this way. Days of prayer and fasting in which the staff and student body took part, although not always easy, were a stimulus to her. On the afternoon of one fast day she walked the miles into Swansea to speak at a Sisterhood, "with only a cup of tea in me from the night before. I was offered food but was not willing to break the fast until the others did . . . The meeting was very good. You can tell the boys that it's true that it's best to preach on an empty tummy! The Lord was there and He blessed."

With those to whom she owed so much—her widowed mother, her spiritual family and Arthur's Mission in Bermondsey—Bessie kept close and faithful contact. For her mother, still living a hand-to-mouth existence, she had a deep and practical concern. Hours she spent in prayer and fasting, pleading with God, shedding many tears for the one she so dearly loved. God spoke to her from Isaiah 42: 16 and gave her the assurance that her mother would believe; but, although faith appropriated the promise, Bessie did not relax the fervency and frequency of her pleadings.

"I fasted lunch and supper, and spent the time in prayer for Mum . . . I had a wonderful time with Him especially concerning Mum. I know the Lord will do something soon."

But her love found ways of expression—the bunch of fresh primroses gathered in Carswell woods, carefully packed and sent home to bring a breath of spring into the high tenement; the prayer for money to give her mother a holiday by the sea and to send her brother for a break to the country; and the personal responsibility she took for the weekly rent for home.

The Lord gave the rent money and I sent it to Mum. Although I asked her to tell me what she thought about loving the Lord she wrote and told me straight she did not want to get religious. Still she will come, in spite of herself.

What do you think? Someone went up to Mum's last Sunday and gave her an envelope with ten shillings in it . . . I prayed all week before that He would send Mum her rent. Praise Him! I am sure she will see His good hand one day.

This week I had a real test. I had a shilling sent to me for my birthday from Flo. I just changed it and sent it back to Mum knowing of her need. Well I had a letter Wednesday saying thanks for it. It came when she hadn't a penny in the house apart from the rent money. You can imagine what I felt like. I had to come up to my room and have a good howl. These days I don't seem able to do much else, I have such a burden for Mum. I pleaded with the Lord to send me ten shillings for the rent this week. I spent nearly three-quarters of an hour on my knees and then a new student came into my room. She did not know my need but went on to tell me about her luggage that had gone to the wrong address. It had just arrived at College, and on unpacking she found a ten shilling note in an old envelope which she did not know she had. She wanted to give it to me she said. So I was delivered in time!

It was good of you to go and see Mum and take her flowers. I wrote her a long letter last week with the ten shillings enclosed but I only received thanks; not a word about the Lord, but I know she will come. I am longing to come home to have another shot at her.

So prayer and faith became two of the principal ingredients in Bessie's life. Her co-students took note of these qualities and remember her by them. As she learned to trust God for personal needs, so He entrusted her with the sharing of what He supplied, and a generous spirit was born within her. One morning the mail brought her a postal order for one shilling. At class time the Principal brought before the students the extreme financial need of the College—he had only a halfpenny in the funds—and Bessie surrendered her one shilling, not without wondering how she was going to get her stamps. Later in the day two gifts cleared the running expenses of the College and Bessie was given back her shilling. It was a test she was not to forget.

I know now from experience that whatever I have given to the Lord He has given back at least a hundred-fold. Yesterday I was given half-a-crown and the word was dropped to me that one of our girls had that amount owing of her last term's fees, so I put it to that. Today your gift was three shillings more than it has been for the last few times. Truly the Lord is no man's debtor. Hallelujah!

It was almost the end of term and her second year was successfully drawing to a close. Her fees were fully paid and she had enough in hand to take her home for vacation where she hoped to have some dental treatment done. A letter was already on its way to her friend telling her to expect her when another one followed it closely merely saying that there was a delay. The untold fact was that a classmate had not been able to complete her fees, and Bessie's fare home was gladly sacrificed.

Within two days her joy knew no limits for not only did she have her fare and money for her dental treatment but even some to spare.

The stirrings of the Holy Spirit are as undetectable as the wind, and His whispers inaudible as the breeze. But the highlights of all Christian experience are those moments of imperishable value which come to the searching, loving heart. And such was Bessie's. She never found it easy to define her spiritual crises—if such they could be termed—but she was sensitive to the Spirit and responsive to His dealings with her. He taught her the meaning of 'full surrender' and 'death to self-life'. He gave her longings after His fullness and answered her desire. He taught her the pre-eminence of Christ in personal experience and moved her heart with compassion for the lost souls of the world. And this all during her three years at College. That is why the Bible College of Wales became to her a place of sacred memory. The Principal and tutors, visiting speakers and missionaries, days of conference and days of prayer, all made their contribution to the forming of this life.

But most particularly Bessie was influenced by the ministry and message of Mr. Norman Grubb of the Worldwide Evangelization Crusade. On his quite frequent visits to the College he laid the world's needs before the student body, challenging them especially with the vast areas of every continent not yet penetrated by the Christian messenger. Bessie looked up to him as a man of ambitious faith whose leadership she would gladly follow. She knew at once that God was wanting her for some unreached part and her longing for overseas service became so intense that at one time she wondered whether or not she should finish the full three years' course at College. Why, if the need were so desperate, could she not quit studies and go? In this she had to learn the discipline of the Spirit, but she was willing. Hearing of the numbers needed and of the targets of faith both for recruits and for finance for the W.E.C. she gave her support in prayer and shared in the triumph of one target reached and a greater one set for the following year. As the months slipped by the question of where she should serve the Lord became more pressing. That the call of God demanded courage and sacrifice and often entailed suffering, she had no doubt.

"You don't go to the mission-field if you can help it, but, if the Lord has called you, you can't help it," she quoted from one of the visiting missionaries. And again, "Nothing but pure love for Christ will get you through the hardships there, but it's a grand life even if it costs." Then God indicated to her that it was to be Africa although, "I am quite willing for India, if He should say so."

With only one term more to go Bessie travelled up to London during her Easter vacation of 1935 and faced the medical examination. Bouts of 'flu and subsequent anaemia had dogged her during her studies, teeth extractions had led to severe haemorrhage, but she knew that before applying as a candidate to the Secretary of the Worldwide Evangelization Crusade, she would have to have a record of physical fitness. So she visited St. Thomas's Hospital quite near to her own Bermondsey home. She admitted that it was quite an experience when the doctor, "went over every inch of me, even my little varicose vein". But his report was favourable with only a supply of pills to help out the blood count.

It was high summer of 1935 when Bessie graduated from the Bible College of Wales and carefully packed in her suitcase her blue uniform dress with all its memories—the deep mauve of the sea on an early sunrise, the dancing bluebells of the Carswell woods, the nervous tension of the first sermon over which she had spent hours of study and still felt uncertain, the precious friendship with her first room-mate, Nan, the moments of sickening loneliness, the ecstasies of answered prayer—packed up they were, but not discarded, for they were the fabric from which the garment of life was yet to be shaped.

4

Bessie rang the bell of Number 17, Highland Road in South East London, and gasped when a maid in uniform opened the door and took her case from her. Stepping into the entrance hall of the Headquarters of the Worldwide Evangelization Crusade, formerly the home of C. T. Studd, she nervously adjusted her hat, drew off one glove and waited, her heart pounding until the first introductions were over and she joined the other missionary candidates.

It was autumn 1935. Not only was Bessie sure that she was called of God to serve Him in Africa but the conviction was growing that it should be in one of the unevangelised areas of the West Coast for which Mr. Grubb had made such stirring appeals during his frequent visits to the Bible College of Wales. Mission policy, formed out of waiting upon God, was that only unevangelised areas not within the intended range of other missionary societies should be entered. Thus the immediate programme of W.E.C. was one of advance into nine unoccupied areas in West Africa, mostly in French-speaking territory. A large wall-map clearly indicated the targets, challenging both staff and candidates in their times of communal morning prayer. Here again Bessie was to learn more deeply the principles of prayer and faith—that in prayer is discovered the will of God, that there is a battle in prayer and a victory in faith when divine assurance is given of a certain answer. So the morning hours were spent, not in household chores and food-preparation, but in bringing specific needs before the Lord, asking Him for men and women recruits, for visas and passages, for health and equipment, for language students and allowances—and, often before the answers came, the song of praise was offered. These were tremendous days for Bessie with the excitement of seeing God do miracles as faith became reality. On her very first day at Headquarters she received a substantial gift which completed her required outfit money of £35. She felt she was a millionaire! Never had she had so much at once. God was surely in her situation and she knew it. This was to be for her the only kind of life worth living—utter dependence upon God, simple faith in His ability to provide for all that He had commanded and restful trust in His guidance.

Then came weeks and months of deputation tours with returned missionaries. The lass from Bermondsey had begun her 'Judea and Samaria' ministry. The team's itinerary took them through the industrial towns of north-west England then over to Ireland. This was Bessie's first experience of sailing, and she expected to be seasick, but was not. She fell in love with Ireland right away, being given hospitality in the home of two ladies.

I have never stayed in a place like this. They are real aristocrats—maids and tea in a most lovely drawing-room, and a grand car driven by a chauffeur who put a rug on me. I had breakfast in bed, brought up by a maid, and then, after coming down, they took me for a drive. We went into the Irish Free State, right up by the Lough into Donegal. My, it was great! I did enjoy it. He truly makes us to reign with princes. Hallelujah!

Back to England and a further series of meetings in the north-west from where Bessie wrote, "We need a fresh anointing of the Holy Ghost every night," where opposition in the form of criticism sent them to prayer and where physical renewal had to be claimed daily. Reporting to her Arthur's Mission family, she wrote:

Last Sunday I had to take the services in a Methodist church. There I was, perched high up in the pulpit and given the order of service and having to preach as well. It was another new experience and I felt really helpless and, just as I stood up, it flashed through my mind that Arthur's had been praying that morning at the prayer meeting. It was a great stimulus to me and the whole day went well. Many told me they had been blessed. Praise Him!

Easter 1936 was approaching and Bessie, now at Headquarters, determined to set time aside for waiting on God to know more definitely His will. For a time the question of her studying French as a next step in preparation was debated and it seemed at one point likely that she would go over to France after doing some preliminary studies in London. Then, out of this time of searching and uncertainty—"I'm just willing for anything that is His will . . . It is better to live just a day at a time . . ."—there came the personal assurance that God was directing her to Portuguese Guinea on the West Coast of Africa. This was confirmed a week later in an interview she had with Mr. Grubb who

called me into his study and told me that on Sunday the Lord spoke to him and told him I was for Portuguese Guinea. I told him how the Lord had led me a week ago and had twice given the word that 'a great and effectual door is open unto you', the one really confirmed the other. I expect this is all a shock to you as in a way it was to me and will even be more so when I tell you that I may sail at the end of June but God will give grace. It's my poor old Mum I think of more than anything and really ask God to give her grace, poor dear. I'm really trusting for her salvation.

A very hurried note on a postcard sent to her friend, Theresa, on 18th May 1936 gave the news of a sailing date in June. Then followed some weeks of quick preparation, a visit to the Bible College of Wales, further tooth extractions and injections necessary for tropical countries, all climaxed by the valedictory service at Arthur's Mission where over two hundred crowded the large upper hall. Mr. Norman Grubb was principal speaker, and there, in the audience, were the members of Bessie's family—Mum, Win and Flo, John and Norman. It was an intensely moving service, when the young missionary recruit, her heart filled with a longing concern, gave no words of farewell but, with all the fervency of the Spirit in her own inimitable way, preached the Gospel.

Next day she said to her mother, "Mum, did you enjoy the meeting last night?"

"Yes, I did," was the reply.

"Mum, don't you feel you'd like to give your heart to Jesus?"

She straightened herself up and said, "Don't you talk to me about religion. Religion has severed you from me."

The sailing date was finally fixed for 27th June from Southampton. Her destination was to be Angola, a Portuguese colony where temporarily she was to help Miss Williamson of the Angola Evangelical Mission. In this way, it was thought, she would gain experience and come to grips with the language. Previously two young men from the W.E.C. had sailed for Angola. They were to precede her into Portuguese Guinea to pioneer the work of that wholly unevangelised land.

Some fifty friends met on the station platform at Waterloo to see Bessie off. Among them were her family, including her mother—the mother for whom she never ceased to pray for yet another thirty years, until at the age of eighty-five and very near to death she finally yielded herself to God. She travelled from London to Southampton with two of her Arthur's friends. Then they boarded the S.S. *Almansora* where her parting words, "Hallelujah for the Cross, Tess" sent them off in different directions to further His cause for a lost world.

The first days on board ship were devastatingly tearful ones despite her repeated efforts not to give in. The batch of letters from home, received when the ship berthed at Lisbon, brought back painful memories. But God had given her friends in the city, who, knowing very little English but understanding the ache of her heart, brought out an English Bible and when they had found John: 15, verse 16, they made her read it aloud to them. Then, in very tenderly-spoken attempted English, they simply said, "He knows."

A few days later Bessie embarked on another ship, the S.S. *Lourenço Marques*, with sixteen sailing days ahead of her to Angola. She now wrote of the peace in her heart and the sufficiency of His grace, although the heat intensified and sickness laid her low.

"I have been sick as usual and wake up most mornings feeling sick. The other night I said to the Captain that I didn't feel like dinner, and, without another word, he rang for the steward and ordered chicken broth and a portion of chicken to be brought out on deck for my supper. Talk about 'the king's daughter', I feel like Joseph of old, finding favour with all."

En route the ship called at the Cape Verde Islands and it was here that Bessie got her first glimpse of 'real Africans'.

"It was amusing to watch three of them in a boat. They had a large fish which the young one was cutting up, just paddling in the blood. Then he hoisted it up to one of the crew who gave him some money and some bread and they sailed away happily."

Towards the end of July Bessie arrived at Cabinda, Angola, her temporary destination. To her consternation, there was no one at the ship to meet her. Her letter to Miss Williamson, warning her of her coming, turned up a week later! What an appropriate introduction to another culture, where delays are common-place and temper western impatience, living is more leisurely and there is a different set of rules. Weeks without mail followed by an avalanche of it bothered Bessie at first.

"I am just hungry for more letters . . . This letter business is a thing I need to get victory in I think. Praise Him that even that will come."

Other introductions soon had to be made, and Bessie, never short of enthusiasm, made her first attempts at riding a bicycle, using a typewriter and learning a language. African roads were not much of a help with the first, nor did the sticky heat facilitate her typing efforts, but language-study she loved, if not the mechanics of grammar, the music of sounds and the joy of communication.

"Miss W. is very kind and gives me plenty of time to study mornings and afternoons. I have one lesson a day with the evangelist . . . How I long to know the lingo . . . As soon as I do I shall be out among the people."

Everyday incidents, always more meaningful to the 'stranger', captured her imagination and often provided great fun. She wrote of the boy who found one discarded sock and insisted on wearing it when he dressed to serve the table. She told of the daily jigger-hunt—little sand fleas no bigger than a pin-head burrow into the skin particularly of the feet and have to be dug out with a needle, otherwise they form a nest and the part becomes intensely irritated. There were the cockroach-chases too.

"At night before going to bed we have a hunt for cockroaches. Miss W. kills them for I haven't got up to that stage yet. They are so huge I haven't the pluck to swash them!" Later she was to have other exciting moments—when three snakes were killed within an hour, when a leopard attacked the village dogs, and when she slept for the first time in an African hut in the bush.

In the month of November Mr. Stober, the Field Leader, returned from Britain after furlough, and to the uninhibited delight of Bessie, brought a radio with him.

The other night we had it on for the first time. Can you imagine what we felt like when we heard the six o'clock Greenwich time-signal and then, 'This is London calling'. London! Yes calling Cabinda as plain as if we were sitting in your home. We fairly danced for joy and it seemed all too good to be true that we even sat and listened to football and cricket because it was so wonderful to be in touch with London . . . The Test Match in Australia too . . .

Last night we again heard London calling and were greatly shocked to hear that the Crystal Palace has been burnt down. What a pity and what a fire it must have been.

When Christmas had come and gone Bessie suddenly realised that not only was it totally unlike anything at home but that she had not even felt homesick. This was all of God, she was sure. She sensed that a battle was over; that the unsettling and disturbing moments of heart-sickness-for-home were put behind; that she was free to move ahead into God's purposes. She began to teach a little in the children's school; not that she felt very capable of doing so as she had still a long way to go in her own language-learning. However, it was a profitable exercise in allowing her closer contact with the Africans and the use of what Portuguese she had assimilated. Then she took a women's class on a Sunday morning.

"I think they all understand the message and I seemed to have more liberty than before, but I still need to know more . . ."

Just as her first Christmas marked an inner victory, so her first Easter in Angola was filled with the joy and exhilaration of spiritual outreach. But let her tell her own story.

I am sure you would like to know the way in which I spent my Easter. Well, I went away to the country. For, as most of you know, our station is by the sea. It was not exactly an Easter holiday but to me it gave more joy than that. We set off on Good Friday by car, of which we had a loan, but it was not exactly a joy ride for these African roads do not always allow one to sit comfortably. However the first part of the road was not so bad, and one could enjoy the beautiful scenery. For several miles of the way the sea was to be seen and the road was just a continual succession of hills and valleys. I wish I could describe to you more of its beauty—the lovely trees and the sea on our left as blue as could be and the sands dazzling white in the sun. Truly one wonders at the hand of the Creator . . .

When we arrived all the Africans came out to meet us. What a sight! Praise His Name, these folk have won my heart. They began to beat the large native drum, which is heard for miles around, to announce that the missionaries had arrived . . . I saw the first large native-built church which could seat about 500 people easily. Braz, the evangelist, was the leader of it; he had the vision of it from the Lord. There are proper forms in it and a pulpit all of the wood they cut from the forest . . . On the day we arrived we had a prayer meeting, but really only a few had arrived from the other towns, some having to walk two days to get here.

On Saturday we walked to another town about three miles away. We went through a bush path with the high grass far above our heads, then through the forest; really it was great and my heart was full of joy.

All day Sunday we had very blessed times . . . In the afternoon I had quite a good time with the women; another woman translated for me into the local language . . . I was also asked to give a word of testimony and the Lord really did help me. I felt His power, praise Him. The evangelist said I did very well with my Portuguese and I was greatly encouraged . . . We partook of the Lord's Supper with over a hundred Africans . . .

To be in an African town like that and to sleep in a native house and really live among them seems to be my Eldorado, and only makes me long for the day when I can get down to it. God is preparing me these days and filling my heart with very big desires for the future. May all that is of Him be not merely desires but reality. The need is all around here to say nothing of Portuguese Guinea and other untouched places.

I have been so blessed in my own soul these days as I have waited upon the Lord. He is the lover of our souls. Continue to pray for me that the Lord may give guidance and wisdom regarding the future.

As she penned these words her thoughts flew to Portuguese Guinea, and it seemed then that a move forward was imminent. Her whole being longed for that land and for that measure of knowing the fulfilment of God's call and purposes for her life. Surely she had served a full apprenticeship in Angola? Her face was set, especially after, for the first time since leaving England, she met the two young men who also were headed for Portuguese Guinea. They had prayer together and discussed the opening up of the new field. The leader of the party already had consent from London to go ahead of the others as soon as shipping and finance were available. But faith and patience were to be tested to the last degree, for, as the months jogged unhurriedly by, one obstacle after another presented itself to hinder and delay. Lines of communication between the field and London became confused, sailing dates were proposed and postponed, severe blackwater fever laid the senior missionary so low that the whole matter of his proceeding to Portuguese Guinea at all was in the balance (utterly unthinkable to Bessie that he should do otherwise), and, most frustrating of all to her, being a woman, she was not to be allowed to join the advance party.

"You don't know how often I feel like wishing I was a man. If I were a man, it wouldn't cost me to go into Guinea, but, as a woman, it has hosts of difficulties; yet I even think if I had the word of the Lord for it, I would go . . ."

For months she lived in this state of unsettledness. But God was in every situation as she was to prove, teaching her the 'grace of patience' and giving her further practical experience in medical work and organ-playing, until her heart was still and she was completely resigned to staying indefinitely in Angola. In fact, she now could see this as 'good and acceptable' for had she not been praying for an outpouring of the Spirit in revival and she had not yet experienced this? Surely then she should stay. She had come to terms with this and had written a letter of explanation to her field leader (although that letter was never posted) when a telegram came from him with 'marching orders'. The three of them were to proceed to the Cape Verde Islands, Portuguese West Africa, to the already established work of the Church of the Nazarene. From there entry would be made by the young men into Portuguese Guinea.

"But *I* shall stay in Cape Verde, being single. My, it seems such a hindrance at times for it is very difficult for a single girl to go about alone, and even more difficult with other men!"

On 12th October a motor-boat took the three pioneer missionaries out from Cabinda to the waiting ship. At that moment Bessie realised how much of her heart she was leaving in Angola as crowds of mothers and children came to wave her off. But two weeks later, after a record voyage when she had known no sickness and had been able to lead a woman passenger to the Lord, she landed with the others at Praia, Cape Verde Islands, to be welcomed by Pastor and Mrs. Howard, American missionaries in charge of the Church of the Nazarene work in the Cape Verde Islands. A new chapter in Bessie's book of life had begun.

5

I ask, O Lord, for patience.
Then, with fretting petulance I cry,
'Why not THEN? Why not THERE?'
I see no reason in Your reasoning.
And, in ceaseless pleading for Your will,
I am too blind to understand that
It is HERE and NOW.
O Lord, forgive.

FROM ANGOLA TO the Cape Verde Islands—the first giant step had been taken. The next one to the mainland of Portuguese Guinea seemed to Bessie relatively short. She was much nearer now, she felt, than in Angola—by twelve days' sea voyage and two long years of waiting. How her heart warmed at the thought of Guinea being so near. How often her thoughts spanned the three hundred separating miles of Atlantic Ocean.

The Cape Verde Islands, nine little fragments broken off from the West Coast of Africa and lying in tropical pleasantness, are inhabited by an industrious and well-educated people, who, by their intermarriage with Europeans, have caught the most attractive features from two continents. Add to these their smartly-tailored suits, their expert blending of colours and materials in dressmaking and their choice of accessories, and you have the kind of people to whom Bessie was now introduced. It seemed a whole new world to her.

Instead of the traditional-style sprawling mission compound she found just a rented house, the home of Pastor and Mrs. Howard and their little girls, a place of love and friendship and laughter. The luxury of a piano, electric light and 'even an icebox' in the home, made life so different for her, and she appreciated every part of it. Many times and many years later, Bessie would explain that it was from Mrs. Howard that she learned how to dress for formal occasions, how to converse with officials and how to remain poised and correct in company. Her wardrobe from then on always included 'a little black dress—you can't go wrong', gloves and a modest piece of jewellery. The girl from London's East End could not be faulted in any society.

The unexpected and the most exciting feature to her was to find a quality of responsiveness to the Gospel that she had not before experienced. On five of the islands there already was an active witness and a growing Church. Meetings were held in homes and in the open air, and, with her Spirit-given ability in Gospel-preaching, she found much opportunity for making her Lord known.

> Last Sunday we had a lovely meeting at the home of a man recently converted. Mr. Howard was ill . . . so I had to be the preacher . . . I felt so weak and nervous . . . The Lord answered prayer as I took the story of the woman of Samaria. The old fire came back which I thought I had lost; my tongue went loose, my arms and all. Best of all, two women stood up and said they wanted to become Christians. One of them is the wife of the owner of the house . . . It was a great encouragement to me.

Among the converts of these early days in Praia was a Cape

Verdian woman, Dona Libania, a dressmaker. An older woman with a grown-up family, she brought much joy to the missionaries through her keenness to learn from the Lord and to witness. Her friendship and fellowship were to mean a great deal to Bessie later on.

By Easter 1939 another young man had come out from England and plans began to take shape for the advance party to go into Portuguese Guinea. But, to her disappointment, Bessie was not included. It was then that the frustration of being a woman and single hit her badly. She complained in prayer and wrote volubly about it to her personal friend! Had she not renounced the thought of marriage to serve God? Now the reverse seemed to be the requirement! What was He doing with her? She compared her situation with that of Mary Slesor—'she knew what loneliness was'—and determined that at all costs she would do His will.

"I have felt tested," she wrote, and that feeling was to persist, for to her frustration and loneliness were added financial strain, fear and physical weakness. Then, the greatest blow of all, the sudden death of her younger sister, Win, seemed to crush her. Her heart was anguished, and homesickness tore her to shreds. Thoughts of her unconverted mother troubled her; and, added to all this, was the fact that war clouds were now hanging low over Europe with all their implications for her brothers and family in London. At times the call to obedience and faith seemed irreconcilable with her own human inadequacy. But the paradox of the spiritual law remains unchanged—out of weakness, strength; out of brokenness, blessing. God deals with us in love, and knows the measure of our capacity.

The first batch of mail from Guinea mainland brought heartening news. The young men had been given temporary hospitality at the home of the British (African) Director of the Cable and Wireless Company. Contacts made on an official level had been favourable and, pending permission from Lisbon for permanent residence and for the work of 'catechising', there were no real limitations put on their efforts in the interim. Meanwhile God had touched the heart of Dona Libania to offer to accompany Bessie to the mainland. The suggestion that she should set up home in Bissau where she had previously worked, earn her living by her dressmaking and share her place with Bessie, was received as an answer to prayer. The third young man then joined the other two, and a provisional date for sailing was set for Bessie and Dona Libania. Then, with the thought of Guinea uppermost in her mind, Bessie accepted a proposal of marriage from the leader of the group. She had known him for a number of years now. She could look back to the time in Angola when she nursed him through his time of severe sickness and felt then the first stirrings towards him. To be married to one who shared her love for Guinea seemed the most wonderful outcome to all her years of waiting, frustration and loneliness.

The first ripples of the European war were beginning to be felt. Mail was often delayed and closely censored. Diminishing stocks meant rising prices. Bessie, alone on the island of Fogo, was disturbed by the reports coming from Bissau. The men were encountering difficulties out of which they could see no way. Government standards for buildings were beyond the usual missionary standards and the team had to be housed before any permanent work could be begun. As no funds for building were then available from British Headquarters, the men felt obliged to withdraw and resign. To Bessie the news was shattering.

"You can imagine what a shock this was to me. I wept and wept when I received the letter. I fasted and prayed and pleaded on the Lord to help them not to leave . . . I thought I had faith, and dared to believe they would stay, now the door to Guinea had been opened to us at last . . ."

After that letter, and with it the request that she should cancel her passage to Guinea, came a telegram intimating the resignation of the three men and their return to Cape Verde Islands.

"I thought my heart would break . . . I cannot describe to you what it all means . . ."

The tension knew no easement when the men returned to Praia. Every day was heavy with decision. Suggestions and solutions came from every quarter—she could stay on the Islands, they could get married, they could take charge while the other missionaries went on leave, she could go to Senegal, she could go to Ivory Coast, they could return to Angola. In the centre of it all was a torn heart.

"This seems to be the biggest test of my life . . . I love him but, as you know, the will of God is first to me . . . Guinea, the land we had prayed for, planned for and sacrificed for, *gone* . . . God has helped me in this great trial . . ."

From the smouldering fires of those weeks of testing, when even the company of her fiancé seemed only to aggravate her distress, there emerged for her two dominating facts—that she could not leave W.E.C., and that she could not give up Guinea. So the engagement of only a few short weeks was broken, and the outlook seemed desolate.

By the time an eventual direction came to her from London, Bessie had fought the lonely battle that was to be the decision of her life-time—that she should go into Portuguese Guinea alone. In her inner struggle she had enumerated all the reasons for not going—her inability with the language, her inability to treat Government papers, the impossibility of her living alone and a woman at that, the question of leadership, the possible attitude of the Government. Apprehension would have made a coward out of her—"but I know that God can look after me and will; all that matters is to do His will". In the weeks of waiting which followed her decision, peace came to her troubled heart, and with the grace of acceptance came the patience of endurance and the strength to move forward into the unknown.

So preparations got under way. Her letters home requested

shoes and a watch, "not a big one, a proper lady's one, reliable
for the tropics . . . might cost quite a lot, probably £3. You
know, something good yet pretty; so many folk think missionaries don't need or like pretty things . . ." Official recognition of
her as the new Field Leader came from London, and the field
accounts and files were handed over to her. It hurt deeply to
have to accept them from the one she had hoped to marry.
From the Senegal field came a rather surprising letter, the
significance of which was scarcely recognisable at the time. It
was from "Mr. Leslie Brierley . . . saying he feels called to take
up the leadership in Guinea . . . He is a fine fellow and will
make a splendid leader, I am sure . . ."

The next important step was to fix the date of her leaving for
Portuguese Guinea. There was the question of further study of
Portuguese in the Islands and a language examination to be
taken. On the other hand, the wet season would soon be settling
in, making a move more difficult. She appealed to the Home
Staff for their decision. If the move were imminent before the
rains, they would have to cable their reply right away. Then she
would make hurried final preparations.

The cable came—she was to enter Guinea before the rains
came. On the 9th May, 1940, she penned these words to her
friend:

I have just received the cable . . . I go D.V. on the 20th
May to Guinea. I can hardly believe it is true and I still have
my fears. NEVER did I need prayer more than I do now. So
don't fail. What shall I say to the Governor? That's one of
the questions I keep asking, but words will be given me for
the hour. Dona Libania is unable to accompany me because
of papers still to be regulated but she will follow in forty
days' time. So I go ALONE, yet NOT ALONE—with HIM. Ps.
121.

But how wonderful God is! How well He arranges what we

leave to Him. He knows our needs—friendship for the lonely, help for the stranger, kindness for the fearful. What a comfort to Bessie to find that travelling on the same ship was the Judge who had been in Cabinda, Angola. He introduced her to the ship's doctor who insisted on her using the first-class deck and who, in turn, introduced her to the Government doctor when the ship reached Bolama, at that time the political capital of Portuguese Guinea. Then as she stepped ashore and was working out her next move, she noticed a young man looking intently at her. She took off her sunglasses to see more clearly. He did the same, and there was an instant smile of recognition. He and his sister had been fellow-passengers with Bessie on the first ship out to Angola. At once there was a helping hand to the customs shed with her luggage. News of her arrival travelled fast to the Director of Cable and Wireless and within minutes he was on the spot taking charge of operations and driving her to the necessary offices where she could regulate her visa, then to the bank and to the hotel. And there, in the hotel, was a fine Christian from Praia, deputy chief of the treasury, who gave up his room for her as the hotel was full and he was on his way that same day to Bissau. Before leaving he saw to it that she had all that she needed and gave her the promise of his help when her ship would berth a few days later at Bissau.

Then came the most important meeting of all, the one she most dreaded, with the Administrator. She turned her well chosen phrases over and over again in her mind all the way to the Government offices, while her handkerchief, screwed up into a little ball in the palm of her hand, became more and more moist. Suppose he proved awkward? Suppose he asked questions she would rather avoid? Suppose he saw through her inabilities and made her feel small? Suppose . . . But all her suppositions came abruptly to an end when, ushered into his presence, she was greeted with the unbelievable words, "How nice to meet you! We have been waiting for you for a long time." There was no need now for pretty speeches. She felt welcomed and wanted. By the time she was shown out of his office, she had arranged for her permit of residence, she had the authority of the Administrator to travel about the country as she wished and she had received the offer of his help whenever required and the prospect of an introduction to the Governor.

That her Father cared and that she was in His will was clear beyond doubt to her now. But how was she ever to begin to evangelise? And how would she fare before the Governor when the time came? There would be the difficulty of accommodation in Bissau too. Houses were scarce and rents very high. How could she hold meetings in rented rooms?

"I feel such a child in everything. I need your constant help in prayer. God has truly answered in a wonderful way far beyond all that I ever dreamed of. I have got into the land, now I must get into the hearts of the people and win them for Christ. This is even more difficult. Love is the way. Pray for me."

6

Bessie sat down at her little portable organ. One pedal was missing, away for repair, but she worked all the more vigorously on the other, squeezing out the three melodies that made up her repertoire—'Count Your Blessings', 'Take the Name of Jesus with You' and 'Let the Lower Lights be Burning'! She had asked Mr. R. of the Wireless Station to be the organist for this first ever meeting in her little room, but what if he did not come? She had better be prepared for the emergency.

Mr. R. did turn up, and so did ten other well-dressed Cape Verdian girls who had been invited. They filled the two improvised pews—a camp bed at the back and two tin trunks in front covered with rugs—and they giggled the whole way through the meeting. To Bessie and her companion it seemed such a fiasco. They were completely at a loss to know what to do. When they had all gone and Bessie was searching in quiet solitude for an answer, a butterfly fluttered in through the open window and alighted on the wall. Seeing in this creation of loveliness the parable of life out of death, Bessie spoke the cry of her heart, "Oh God, there must be a resurrection. You are going to build Your Church in Portuguese Guinea."

Yet for these first few months nothing seemed more unlikely. Bessie had arrived at Bissau in May, but before Dona Libania had joined her at the end of June, she had been tempted a thousand times to give up. She found the heat very oppressive at the beginning of the wet season. How often she would change her sticky clothing in a vain attempt to find a little coolness and comfort. How often she had taken refuge from physical exhaustion on her bed.

"I feel just fit for nothing," she wrote during her first days to her friend. But, with a hotel bill eating into her scant resources, she made the effort to get around, and within a week had found rooms to rent at £3 a month—"Everything is *so* dear"—and was finding her way about town. Shopping at Bissau prices proved a formidable task, while thinking and conversing solely in Portuguese increased her feeling of strangeness.

Not surprisingly, she fell victim to a prolonged attack of malaria with such recurrent sickness and violent headaches that she finally had to call in a doctor. When the fever had abated ugly depression took over. She wept for her loved ones so far away under war conditions. Her lonely heart cried for friendship and grieved over her broken engagement. She felt that her courage had ebbed away completely. Time and again she asked so many questions of God, the how and the why of His dealings with her then seemed so inexplicable, but she found a source of comfort in His promise that He would not quench the smoking flax nor break the bruised reed. Oh how bruised she felt! What could the outcome of such inauspicious beginnings be, she wondered? That she had to leave with the Lord who in His grace brings us to nothingness, and then constructs His edifice on our ruins.

A return visit to Bolama enabled her to get her residence card and to have her first interview with the Governor who was more helpful than she had imagined. He put her at ease at once, and she found to her delight that she was able to say the right things, in the right way, at the right time.

The wet season was almost at an end for that year when news trickled through from London that a missionary couple, who had been scheduled for another West African country, were planning to do a preliminary spell in Portuguese Guinea. The thought of their arrival heartened Bessie tremendously, and her immediate concern was for larger accommodation. By November she and Libania had moved into a three-roomed house with bathroom and scullery, and were awaiting the re-inforcements.

With the new move, numbers to the meetings increased until as many as thirty would gather on Thursday and Sunday evenings. When all the available seating proved inadequate an African carpenter was given an order for three wooden benches. Over the months the town had been well covered with evangelical literature, gospels had been sold and several Bibles had found their way into homes.

On one occasion Bessie was able to make a trip well into the interior where she visited a number of Balanta towns and villages. She was thrilled with what she saw and felt that eventually she would settle among the tribespeople just as soon as someone else came to take responsibility for the work. She was not too far away from Senegal and the small missionary group there in the Casamance, the southern region of that country. From time to time they were able to exchange news through African friends who often covered the distance between the stations on foot. On her first Christmas Bessie was able to send them a parcel of goodies from the big city as their village station was well away from sources of supply.

Before her first anniversary in Bissau, the lone missionary pioneer was beginning to see the longed-for results of her year's work—people were being converted to Christ. As she preached week by week in her little sitting-room, her lips would be touched with holy fire. Words would flow with an ease that surprised her. When she related Bible incidents, they became alive. Bessie was a gospel preacher and her appeals were always passionate. She never failed to urge her listeners to get right with God, to stay behind after the meeting and pray if they wished to do so. One night Mimi stayed. She was the first. She had been a woman of the streets, a harlot and a sorceress. That night as she knelt in prayer and confession God got hold of her and made her new from within. The following week her eighteen-year-old son came to the house saying that he too wanted to get right with God. Later on her second son did the same. Then one evening Mimi brought a friend to the meeting. He was a hugely-proportioned, very black African and was all the more remarkable in his very white suit. He sat right at the front of the meeting, his eyes never leaving Bessie's face, listening intently to her every word. From then on he became a regular attender, his heart strangely warmed and moved by all he heard. Several times he asked if such truths were really to be found in the Bible for he had never heard such a message. Then one night he too stayed behind, prayed for forgiveness and became a child of God. What a transformation! Light had met with darkness and conquered it. In time Sr. A.S. became a powerful preacher, a trusted leader in the Church and a Bible expositor. But at first he walked the Via Dolorosa with a Roman Catholic wife who refused to communicate with him any longer. She would cook his meals but he sat alone at table.

Others too made an open confession of their faith while many lingered near decision. Thus the Church was beginning, taking shape, being built from the fragments of a broken spirit. Bessie loved people because she loved her Lord, and she loved this little spiritual family—'my first-born'—which month by month was growing in number.

But what could be happening to the promised reinforcements? Bessie had been to the Governor and had received his permission for their entry, but there was no mail from England informing her of what was going on. In February one stray letter dated October reached her with news which was, of course, already stale. It was not until July that the first mail for nine months got through and then it was eighty letters in one consignment! What hours of pleasurable reading they gave to her starved soul. There was news from home—of her

brother and brother-in-law becoming Christians, of relations
and friends who had been called into the Forces, of provision
for her mother of accommodation outside of London. It took
her ages to go through them all and to grasp all that they said to
her. To her dismay, there was no word of the awaited couple.

World War II was now pushing its way beyond the frontiers
of Europe. It was difficult not to be involved. Twice Bessie was
called in to help when survivors from British ships were picked
up off the coast and brought into Bissau. It was then that the
British Consul requested her to give some time in the office,
and, although rather diffident at first, she realised that many of
her co-patriots had no other choice but to participate in the war
effort, and so she agreed to do what she could in the circumstances. She had not been trained in secretarial work and found
it hard going, but the money she earned not only helped in her
work but also enabled her to contribute a goodly sum each
month to her mother.

On another occasion, when a group of thirty-five Norwegian
survivors came ashore in lifeboats, her services were again
called for. She gave unstintingly to these men, sparing herself
no effort to meet their needs for the time that they were in port.
When they had gone she found a lovely radio installed in her
room and ready for use, a mark of their appreciation.

So, as in all life, the months passed by patterned with beauty
and bewilderment, ecstasy and agony. One morning a Portuguese friend with whom Bessie had a language exchange
system, sent round a beautiful bunch of red roses, freshly
picked from her garden. It was Bessie's mother's birthday and
the bouquet was a token of affection and friendship which remained throughout all her years. The flowers were lovingly
arranged around her dear one's photograph, but a tear trickled
down on to the fragrant blooms that morning.

Again and again God remarkably blessed the meetings. Bible
study and prayer became the food of the little group of Christians. Yet there were problems, not the least when dear Libania

had a serious heart attack and her stay in Guinea was threatened. Nor did there ever seem to be any progress in the sending out of the promised reinforcements. Bessie attempted through the British Consul to hurry on their visas but without success. And while great joy was evidenced in her work, yet there was the nagging longing to see some of her loved ones and to be relieved from her single-handed responsibility. Then a most unexpected thing happened.

The Vichy-French authorities in Dakar ordered the three missionaries, David and Margaret Barron and Leslie Brierley, out of Senegal giving them only fifteen days to clear the country. Leslie sent a telegram through to Bessie saying that all three were on their way to Bissau.

"I was working in the Consulate's Office at the time and literally danced for joy."

Days of sheer bliss followed as they shared together in her work, meeting the little group of Christians in a fellowship where language is no barrier. The Senegal team had come from an area which had proved almost unfruitful, and it was a spiritual tonic to them to see what God had done in Bissau. Bessie got to work at once to procure permits for them to stay on and help her. There had been a change in Governorship, however, and the request was not granted. They were told quite summarily that they would have to leave on the first available ships. There could be no appeal against the decision.

Margaret Barron takes up the story:

The day came when we were told that we would have to leave Portuguese Guinea. To Bessie it was a terrible blow, her heart seemed as if it would break, she was to be alone again. Leslie was to go on a boat to Sierra Leone and David and I to Lisbon, then on to London. I well remember the day we left. I had seen in her home the faces of those whom she had led to the Lord shine as they sang His praises, and I had wept. Now, as we left, tears were streaming down Bessie's cheeks. The boat pulled out and we were on our way, but dear Bessie was left alone.

Leslie Brierley adds, "We were given twenty-four hours to get out of Portuguese Guinea. It was on that day that a motor launch of the British Government from Sierra Leone steamed in on a courtesy visit. The Consul asked permission of the Captain for me to sail. That's how I got to Sierra Leone."
To Theresa Bessie spilled out her heart in a letter.

Dear, I don't know what I shall do alone. It is almost too much for me. Dona Libania also leaves on the 25th of this month for she has a very weak heart and must return to the Islands. I can't tell you all that this has meant to me. I had hoped that at least Leslie Brierley would have been able to stay, but all had to go. I may also leave if I find it impossible to carry on here alone. My nerves are all upset and I don't sleep at nights. If it were not for the dear Christians around me, I too should go on this ship.

In her extremity, Bessie was further weakened by fever, becoming so ill that the British Consul became alarmed for her. He took the responsibility of cabling to London Headquarters advising them to get her home at once. But as soon as the fever let up Bessie was not easily persuaded to go home! What strange creatures we are! Home seemed so far away and the fear of the work folding up in her absence was all too real. If she went war conditions might prevent her returning for a very long time. She was in a dilemma. Could there not be some kind of compromise for her health's sake—a short break, not too far away? Her thoughts flew to Sierra Leone with its more tolerable climate and its hills, and she was attracted. Had not Leslie Brierley cabled to her from there on his arrival? Had not his subsequent letters to her telling her of the life there and the friends whom he had made thrilled her? But first she must ask for an interview with the Governor and obtain his assurance that there would be no hindrance to her returning after her convalescence. Once she had that, her mind was at rest. She sent a cable off to Leslie asking if he thought the climate of Sierra Leone would help her to recuperate. His reply clinched the matter. She would go—and come again.

The thought of parting from her 'family' became more poignant every day. It would be only for a short time, she told herself. Yet the Spirit was witnessing that it was not so. When the actual sailing date was announced she felt that she could not bear to be away from her group of infant Christians. What could she do for them? How could she best prepare them for her absence? Every evening of the week before she left she gathered them around her, instructing them as carefully and as fully from the Bible as she could. From their number she elected a leader, Sr. A.S., the first man to be converted. Bessie confessed that she did not know what title to give to him, so they named him 'President'. A younger man, who had proved himself in preaching, was chosen as the evangelist, and another who had been well educated became church secretary so that he could write regular reports to Bessie on all that was happening within the Church. They found a little room where they could worship and Bessie paid the rent in advance for the first month. Her furniture she put in store for safe keeping with a Portuguese friend. So she left her babes, some sixteen of them now, to fend for themselves. She had arrived in weakness, she was leaving in weakness. That little group seemed so defenceless.

"Oh God, You are the Almighty One, and we are Yours."

7

Leslie Brierley had a reputation for taking notes, writing reports, keeping a diary and stock-piling information! His personal diary of events from his brief stay in Bissau till his arrival in Freetown, Sierra Leone, explains the situation now arising.

Oct. 9th '41   Bissau, P.G.—

One day a telegram came refusing us permission to stay in Portuguese Guinea. That was unexpected as I had become pretty confident that we could stay. So we prepared to go. Suddenly one day Bessie came in to say there was a boat in the harbour and I could have a passage on her if I could be ready in three hours' time. I had first of all to make up my mind whether to go to Freetown or Lisbon—not such an easy choice under the circumstances. Then, when I had made my choice I had to prepare. But by 5 p.m. we were sailing out of Bissau harbour, having said goodbye to Bessie, with a heavy heart, for I knew it meant leaving her to herself, and also meant leaving one I had learnt to love although I had not told her! And I was going to Freetown—Bessie had lent me £6 . 10 . 0 and I had £4 . 10 . 0 of my own. I knew only one Methodist Minister friend somewhere in Sierra Leone—and that was all! War-time too! Truly it was going out in faith. I could have waited a few days and gone home via Lisbon with the Barrons. It was the dividing of the ways—in more sense than one. The Royal Navy helped me down, and, apart from a little sickness, I had a splendid voyage. Two days later, Sunday, we steamed into Freetown and a new phase in my life began.

Oct. 1941 Freetown, Sierra Leone.

In Freetown, I discovered that my friend, Stanley Brown, was stationed up country and so the only hope I had, failed. A strange land, and strange folk. Only one contact, a Mr. Colman, who was on some war job—I didn't know what—was extremely kind to me and introduced me to Dr. Musselman whom he described as the 'father of all missionaries'. And there I found a home and parents for five months—till someone else took me in charge! My first task when things settled down was to wire Bessie that I had arrived. After much thought I tacked the word 'LOVE' on the end, and, from subsequent information, it seems that that did the trick! From that time I ached for the first letter, and in my turn I wrote in diary form every day, posting it periodically.

It was then that Bessie, having already received Leslie's cable with the first hint of love, sent a cable to him with the suggestion, backed by her doctor's approval, that a change of climate would be beneficial for her health. Leslie could not have agreed more, and what better place than Freetown? In his second cable he had the audacity to append the words, 'Longing to see you'.

From that moment on Bessie exchanged the cup of heartache, loneliness and physical weariness for one of overflowing joy. In Freetown she found a welcoming missionary group, relaxation and relief, the fellowship of which she had felt starved, the opportunity to converse in English, and, above all, the very real love of Leslie and his proposal of marriage.

On the recommendation of the Home Staff, Leslie had

already found employment as a Government Liaison Officer in Sierra Leone, his knowledge of West African tribes and their languages being an undoubted advantage. He was often on reconnaissance trips into the interior, a job for which he had a flair, and one which was to prove a preparation for his future ministry.

The following weeks were spent in a whirlwind of activity, for a cable from England gave her mother's consent and blessing, and there seemed no point in delaying the wedding. Bessie's birthday, the 3rd February, was not too far away and it appeared an appropriate time for celebration. So the date was fixed, until it was discovered that Leslie's friend, Stanley Brown, who was to be best-man, had to leave again on the 3rd for his inland station. At first Bessie and Leslie thought of going with him on a honeymoon ride, but they were soon dissuaded from this by Stanley himself. The wedding was arranged for 2nd February, 1942.

It must be seldom that a bridegroom is ever asked or has the opportunity to describe his immediate pre-wedding days, his bride and the full wedding ceremony. Leslie may not be unique in this, but his letter home to his sister Elsie must surely be unrivalled. In it there is reference to his brother Eric who had been asked to send out the rings.

Battenburg House,
Freetown,
March 3rd, 1942.

My dear Elsie,

You are anxiously waiting some description of the wedding, I presume, from a letter I received yesterday. Ladies always were curious about these things, weren't they?

Well I want to begin at the beginning so I must tell you that away in Portuguese Guinea when I met Bessie for the second time (the first time was in London) there were three things which struck me about her—firstly the wonderful way she had fixed up her little three-roomed house out of a W.E.C. income. It was very nice and comfortable, and so spick and span. Then, on our first day there, it was the regular mid-week meeting; and to see her that evening lead that meeting and all in Portuguese was a tonic to us who had been in a dry and barren land for so many years. To think that she had come in all alone, unknown and without a Christian friend in that land to meet her or to help and advise her. She had started that meeting on her own and had made such progress as to be able to arrange for two meetings a week where above twenty folk would attend regularly and about seven of them had already professed conversion. No ordinary individual could have done it! Thirdly, to go down town with her and see the way she carried everything off, meeting the great of the land as though she were their equal, which she was, to watch her working in the Consulate without any previous experience and being highly commended for her efficiency . . .

All these things made me realise that even though she was run down and not the Bessie we had heard of in England yet she was not one to be left on one side! She was more mature than she was in England, had been through trials and disappointments which had made her into a woman of experience. Then to crown all—and this is where we males go down flat—she came walking out in the evening, after the work of the day was done, in a lovely sort of house-gown which reached to her ankles and fitted her perfectly. She looked a dream! The little bit of powder on her face just put the finishing touches to it all—and down your little brother fell! Of course you and I had been taught that powder was of the devil, but it didn't seem very devilish! Of course she does not powder up or paint her lips as worldly women do, not at all. Bessie is not worldly. Her greatest desire in life is to get back into Portuguese Guinea and help in the building of the little

Church there. But she can discriminate between what is essentially worldly pride and what makes her more, shall we say, womanly and lovable. But you are a woman so I had better shut up or you will be telling me to do so, for I understand that women do not like to hear others of their species being extolled . . .

I need not go into the details of our engagement . . . but the lady accepted. A little later we had a cable from her mother wishing us both joy. So everything was set for the wedding. I suddenly found that it was Bessie's birthday on the 3rd February and that my friend, Stanley Brown, would be down in Freetown just before this. It would be great to have Stanley as best-man, so the date was arranged for 3rd February, (then Stanley altered it to the 2nd).

Bessie then had to begin rushing around buying dress material, shoes and everything else that a lady requires for such an occasion. She was delighted to find she could buy a veil in town, so she had her desire—a white wedding just as she would have had at home. And she is worthy of the best! Her dress was full length and made by a local dressmaker. For her going-away outfit we bought a lovely blue material, and she had blue shoes to match. Bessie then insisted that I get a new suit, so off we went around town again to choose a cloth, a nice grey one with a sort of stripe running through it. Then we had to get shoes for me—£2 a pair for shoes, wicked ain't it? At last we were all fitted up. Then I did what Bessie called a mad thing. I went up country on tour in connection with the job I am doing. I extended the tour so that by the time I got back it was only ten days off our wedding day, and we had no ring. Eric had not got the others out in time so we had to go and order one from a goldsmith in town. He made a very nice one out of real Sierra Leone gold. Indeed, you would not think that it was native made if you did not examine it closely.

By the time I got back home Stanley had already arrived

in Freetown. It was the first time I had seen him for about six years. He was a brick and made all the arrangements for me. He suggested a honeymoon at Leicester Peak, where the Bishop of Sierra Leone has a rest-house, rather than spend four days in a dirty old train going to his station up country.

THE DAY arrived. I had been informed by the bride that I must on no account see her until she came into the church at the time of the ceremony—and she was to dress in MY lodgings! So she had to keep to her room while I was around and I had to shout to let her know where I was!

It was a hot day, and a hot time of day, and the heat of the circumstances added to the discomfiture for I had never been married before! At 1.45 p.m. Stanley and I got into a car and drove off to the United Brethren Church in Regent Road. We sat there in the pew, watching the guests arrive and talking about everything and anything. Then the officiating minister arrived, Dr. Musselman, the Superintendent of the United Brethren in Sierra Leone. He was to take the actual ceremony and the Bishop of Sierra Leone was to give the address. But something went wrong—the Bishop forgot his clerical robes and rushed off for them after having brought the guests to the church—and made himself late, so, in his nervousness, Dr. Musselman had to improvise a speech at the appropriate juncture in the ceremony.

But I'm going before myself. The bride was late. At last the organist struck up 'Here comes the Bride' and we stood to attention. Down the aisle she came slowly on the arm of the Rev. John Kennedy, Superintendent of the Assemblies of God Mission, and accompanied by Miss Hoerner, Secretary of the United Brethren Mission. The bride carried a bouquet of pink flowers, and when she arrived at the altar she gave her bouquet and gloves to her bridesmaid. Then it started. I just felt as though I were a thousand miles away looking at the whole thing through a powerful telescope. When the time came for my statements I made them rather nervously at first but afterwards my voice picked up and I said the things after Dr. M. quite clearly. Bessie was a little quieter, which is not usual. When at last I put the ring on to the lady's finger and we were pronounced man and wife, what a feeling it gave me! Even yet I don't always feel married, it seems as though it is too strange to be true. Anyway we were husband and wife and we went off into the vestry to sign on the dotted line. Mr. Kennedy, who is a singing evangelist, sang a lovely solo while we were busy with the register, and Stanley claimed his right to kiss the bride. I had forgotten that part of the contract! Then I suddenly decided it was time I did my stuff, so I did it. Then we had to face the walk back up the aisle—gracefully and slowly (I wonder)—to the waiting taxi.

Tea was provided by Mrs. Musselman with sandwiches, American cookies and ice-cream. Finally, Bessie and I cut the three-tier cake which Mrs. Kennedy had baked. The trimmings—angels, bells et cetera—were loaned to us by the Sister in the Catholic Convent.

At long last we were free to go, our destination being Leicester Peak where we spent a week just relaxing and lolling around. We had time for only two meals a day. The games we took with us were never played and the books in our cases were never read. It was so new and . . . I had better leave the rest to your Lancashire imagination.

To crown our wedded bliss, a few days after coming back to town we both fell ill and had to go to bed, while Mrs. Horstead, the Bishop's wife, acted as nurse. I got better slightly and returned to work, but Bessie got a further infection—gingivitis—and so we decided to let her have a week at the Princess Christian Hospital . . .

So from the happiness of a honeymoon in the hills to the misfortune of hospitalisation with a severe mouth infection which was no doubt aggravated by her poor state of health. But hospital spelt rest, and with her bed out on the verandah and over-looking the sea, Bessie knew the benefit of those nine days of enforced separation.

Just a few nights after she had come out of hospital they were disturbed from sleep. To their horror, when they had switched on the light, they saw two great black feet peeping out toes upwards from the bottom end of the bed. The thief had already taken quite a haul out on to the verandah and had come back for more. Leslie gave chase, held him for a while but his well-oiled body ensured his escape. He shot through the window and made off. The incident thoroughly unstrung Bessie whose nerves for some time had been out of order.

From her letters it is evident that Bessie's thoughts were never far away from the struggling group of believers in Bissau. Her main concern was to get well and to get back to them. Indeed, Leslie explains that his proposal of marriage was con-ditional—on Bessie's part—that he would return with her to the land of her love. To use his words, he 'married a country as well as a girl'. Yet, ill-health dogged her until at last she had to submit to the decision that they would return to England as soon as a replacement for Leslie had come out.

Their plan for going home did not, however, exclude them from serving God with great enthusiasm where they were. They made a three-week trip to the interior on Government business but took the opportunity at the same time of visiting several mission stations and ministering there. Back in Free-town they were able to rent a good-sized flat where they gave hospitality to the troops calling in at the port. Along with the American missionaries, they took their turn in organising meet-ings and times of fellowship for the serving men.

"Yesterday we had an interesting time when we had two Privates and a Lieutenant for tea, all three of them Christians. Two others came in in the evening. We had a sing, reading, and several expressed their thoughts. We finished with a time of prayer. We surely do feel the Lord is using our home and that is what we want.

"On Saturday evenings we go up the hill to the home of Mr. and Mrs. Birch of the American Wesleyan Mission, and there we entertain quite a number from all ranks. We have hymns and prayer, some games and refreshments which the three missionary families help to provide. The men do enjoy it and I'm sure are blessed."

It was then that a very tempting offer to stay on in Sierra Leone was made to them by another missionary society. The matter momentarily claimed their attention, but Bessie's physical condition and her burning love for Portuguese Guinea enabled them to turn it down.

Almost seven months after Bessie's departure from Bissau, longed-for news of the Church trickled through. It was brought by an African friend on a journey for business reasons. He told how the group were meeting regularly, witnessing and remaining loyal. A further two months were to pass before she received her first written reports from the Church secretary and greetings from the members. The encouragement which these letters brought was tremendous.

The replacement for Leslie was delayed for yet some months. Bessie got busy with her knitting needles meanwhile—she would soon be needing warm woollies for the English winter ahead, and for the expected baby. Early in December their ship docked at Liverpool. Before the end of 1942 there had been a series of introductions and reunions, in Lancashire, in London and at Arthur's Mission.

8

WHO EVER SAID that he would like to be a missionary on furlough? First furlough for Bessie and Leslie added up to two long years of travel in public transport under war conditions with baby Norman Leslie to care for, living from suitcases in a multiplicity of homes and taking part in hundreds of meetings and conferences. A glance at their itinerary for 1943–44 reveals a formidable list of place-names zigzagging the country from Bristol to Colchester, from London to Glasgow, including the Midlands, Yorkshire and the North-West.

The story of Portuguese Guinea—of God's power demonstrated in human weakness, of God's answer to trembling faith, of God's triumph in response to willing obedience—stirred the Christian public all over Britain, for Bessie had the gift of holding her audience in wrapt attention, having them at one instant rippling with laughter, then reducing them to tears of love and shame. She made every scene live, every incident vivid with reality, every appeal deep with emotion. The result was that many were challenged by her experiences. In one report, for example, she wrote, "At Manchester several hundred stood up as I made the appeal."

Leslie's ministry was different. A student and investigator par excellence, his talks were thoughtful studies of the geographical and ethnic situations in West Africa. He produced

60

maps and quoted statistics. He highlighted needs and outlined programmes. He visited libraries wherever he went and during his furlough years he compiled and published a survey of the prevailing missionary position in the world. This 'Black Spots' survey showed up areas of need which became the W.E.C. targets for the following years.

And while God was moving people to pray in Britain, He was keeping watch over His children in Portuguese Guinea. They wrote to their 'Sister Pastor' telling her how they met to read the Word of God and pray each week. The Scripture Gift Mission had made a timely and generous gift of Scripture portions, and the believers had distributed these in all the main towns of the Colony. In such dire poverty, they had proved the abundance of His grace and they were abounding in works of faith and rejoicing in His steadfast love. So greatly heartened were the Brierleys by this first news report that they wrote, "We pray and believe that when we return we shall find much fruit to God's glory from this ministry."

"When we return . . ." The thought of their return was always very present with them, and their applications for visas were lodged with the expectation of a sailing date before the end of the first year. But faith is challenged. "We believe that when we return"—the statement had been made. Now faith both for their visas and for the young Church was tested. The next news from Bissau was of the closing of the meeting-place by the authorities because Sr. S. had no recognition from the Government to conduct religious meetings.

"We are not feeling discouraged because of the difficulties," wrote one of the Portuguese Guinea Christians at that time, "rather do we experience the power of the Holy Ghost Who helps us forward on the Way of Salvation."

January of 1944 crept in and although hopes for an early sailing were still high, the necessary visas were not yet on hand. During the Spring of the year London suffered almost nightly visits from Hitler's war machines, and Bessie, 'a little tired of this trotting round the globe', was torn between the concern for her London family and the desire to be on her way again. "How we long for that boat to come," she wrote to her friend. "Perhaps the Lord is waiting for me to stop grumbling."

The 'grumbling' stopped with good news from Bissau and from David and Margaret Barron. The Christians from Bissau wrote:

We pray our bountiful Father that He would give you, by faith in Christ Jesus, health and happiness, and that this message might arrive soon to give evidence that we are still here, longing for you and your wonderful teaching which we so much need. In our daily prayers, which we continue as always, we have asked the Lord to give a sure date for your return. We await anxiously, but with firm faith, that our prayers will be answered. We are alone, but still looking forward to better days that the Father and His divine Son have reserved for us when you come.

We here, by the will of God, are determined to follow in His way, according to the teaching of Scripture and its growth in us as planted by you. We daily read our Bibles following the Scripture Union portions. We were not able to have a public meeting at Easter because of the decree closing the Church, but we were with you in spirit at the time. We remember that Christ makes Himself felt in the life of each believer, making in him His holy habitation, therefore by His most precious blood He has power for all things.

The Sunday services are functioning separately in the city in the house of Mimi, and in the native quarters in the house of Brother Vaz, as we told you before.

David and Margaret Barron had returned to their former station at Kounkanne, Casamance, Senegal, early in the year. They had found their home in a dreadful state. It was overgrown with weeds, dirty, a shambles. But hard work had changed the face of things and already a missionary outreach had recommenced and a little group of believers was forming.

It was then that another plan of entry came to mind. Why should the Brierleys not go back to Kounkanne, Leslie's previous station, which was only a short distance from the Portuguese Guinea border? Once there, they could make further attempts at procuring their visas, and from Kounkanne to Bissau was only a short hop. Thus the next requirement was French visas for Senegal; and their application was duly made.

Still the difficulties seemed to mount with the months. The shipping company informed them that children were to be prohibited from travelling because of danger on the high seas. That ruled Norman out. This of course was a challenge to Bessie for her treasured offspring was not going to be left behind. So she set about 'obtaining the promises' as she had been so often taught in W.E.C., and to Leslie's consternation, appropriated the phrase 'not a hoof shall be left behind' as her basis of faith that Norman should go with them in spite of the Government wartime decree.

With the bombing of London becoming more persistent they sensed a responsibility to give help at Headquarters. They were there when a flying bomb fell on the road just a few hundred yards away and a stick of bombs tore off doors and broke windows in the property. If it had not been for the protection of a large drawing board over Norman in his cot he would have been riddled with glass splinters.

Then the Crusade Home Secretary wrote to all the missionaries waiting to go overseas saying that, because of the great number on the furlough list who desperately needed a break as soon as conditions allowed, those at home were being asked to find their own passage money. Bessie was shocked. Three passages? When would they ever get back? But on that very day an elderly lady put a £1 note into an envelope with a note saying,

"For your passage or personal." Faith was quickened. Within two weeks an anonymous gift of £50 further strengthened their expectancy.

It was early October and the family was in Glasgow. Bessie had even started a few French lessons. With many meetings in the area, their programme was full when a telephone call from London offered them passages leaving Liverpool on the 2nd November. Neither of them was even in at the time. Leslie was at a meeting in Greenock and Bessie had gone to take a nurses' meeting. But the delay in replying was soon rectified, triggering off a series of hurried preparations. Farewells had to be said, heavy baggage to be sent off, last-minute packing had to be done, meetings to be cancelled, photographs to be taken, prayer-circulars to be written and posted, extra cases to be borrowed—and then all was ready. The day before sailing, Leslie rang the Portuguese Consul in a final appeal for their visas, but he could not give them. There had been no authorisation from Lisbon. And Bessie returned a clothing-coupon book to her friend, Theresa, a reminder that war conditions and clothes-rationing still prevailed, and a token of Theresa's willingness to sacrifice her personal clothing ration to complete her dearest friend's outfit. Bessie had wanted badly to get one more new dress and had hunted exhaustively for something suitable to wear in the tropics, but she had to leave without finding one —so she returned the book, confident that soon enough she would have one run up for her by one of her dressmaker friends in Bissau from a length of unrationed material!

So from the cold of English winter, the fog of Liverpool and its grey skies, they set sail for West Africa, for Senegal and the Mission Station at Kounkanne where David and Margaret Barron were waiting to welcome them and where a two-roomed, low-roofed, mud-brick 'villa' became their temporary home. For Leslie it was, in a sense, coming home for he had helped to build this first station amongst the Fulacounda people. But for Bessie, it was her first real taste of 'bush' life in

West Africa, and her stumbling attempts to say a few words of greeting in the Fula language brought a riot of laughter from her new friends.

While Bessie busied herself making a Christmas cake from the ingredients which she managed to bring with her, Leslie filled in more application forms for visas—through the Consulate at Dakar, through the British Consul in Bissau—even making an appeal for help in the matter through the Chief Civil Administrator who had befriended Bessie in her beginning days in Bissau.

9

"ONE THING WE have learned—that God has a time for everything and in God's time everything is perfectly done."

Dazzling heat lay over the land. The motionless air was cruelly dry. The baked earth cried out for the miracle of rain. Day after day it was the same—and living creatures waited in the shadows till the sun had gone.

Every possible application had been made for visas, but every likely source—London, Dakar, Bathurst and Bissau—had proved an exasperating mirage. Not a sign from any direction, not even a tiny cloud of promise for weeks and months. Where was the God of miracles? Why were the 'heavens as brass'?

But the miracle of rain did come . . . about mid-May, and in God's time. Only a few drops at first, but a certain indication that the parched earth would soon be transformed, that the seed would be sown and that a harvest could be expected.

A letter came from Mr. Grubb with the suggestion that Bessie herself should go down to Bissau and see the Governor. "Is he out of his senses?" she ejaculated in her forthright manner. "Could anyone imagine anything so crazy as trying to cross a frontier without a visa?" But the challenge stuck—to be thought over and rejected time and again.

Not surprisingly the conversation in the 'small house' at Kounkanne had a habit of turning to Portuguese Guinea and visas.

One day while Bessie was busying herself with the chores, Leslie suddenly startled her with the words, "If only I knew Portuguese well enough, I'd go myself to Guinea and see what could be done." Like a flash of illumination the thought came to her, "Well, I have the language, why don't I go?" But just as quickly doubts, fears and questions crowded in on her. The more she thought into the idea, the more ridiculous it seemed—and the clearer came the assurance from God that this was what she should do! For a little time she said nothing. She just prayed and prayed, the conversation private between herself and God. Then, making Leslie's willingness to let her undertake the journey her sign, she voiced the proposal.

"I shall never forget Leslie," she testified years later. "He said, 'Mummy, I could never ask you to do this. But if God has told you, then you must do it.'"

For two further weeks Bessie and Leslie made every detail a matter of prayer. She would have to leave little Norman. She would have to obtain a pass from the French Commandant to take her over the frontier to the first Portuguese Customs Post. The rains had already begun, there were some twenty miles to the Post and they had no transport. How God delights in such situations!

Margaret Barron offered to look after Norman, and the French Commandant not only gave a pass immediately but offered his own car as transport and himself as driver. With that settled, the decision was made. For a second time Bessie was going to enter the land—alone.

Leslie came with me so far—just to the frontier. Will I forget the moment he left me! My Portuguese seemed to leave me also at this time, for not having practised for nearly four years, I could hardly speak a clear sentence at first. I just felt weak and helpless in the frontier village of Pirada. There were three shops in the village each with a European in charge. They told me they expected a lorry for Bafata the next day, but I waited five days for one. Was I tested? All sorts of fears possessed me. Why shouldn't I go back? If an official should come and find me without a visa on my passport, I could close the door to Guinea for ever. What wild scheme had I undertaken? I thought of walking back, but I did not want to do that, I wanted to go forward. One day I even sat on a horse, and thought I could do that bit (to Bafata) on horseback. But, I said to myself, like David of old, "I haven't proved it", and so decided to let the bony beast alone! Then the Lord spoke to me through the story of Esther. It is wonderful how such words stand out like letters of gold as though they were written for oneself alone. God showed me that my petition would be accepted as hers was before the King. She did a risky thing—but God undertook. This was a great encouragement to me. On the fifth day a lorry came. I sat in the front with the driver, and that night we arrived in Bafata.

In Bafata I had to present myself to the Administrator to show my papers. After much prayer I went in to see him. I told him I had been in Portuguese Colonies for six years, that I had left my furniture in Bissau with a friend who was no longer able to look after it for me. (This was true. She had written to say that she was leaving and wanted to know what to do with my belongings.) Then I asked his permission to go on to Bissau to see to the matter. I did not tell him the main reason, but then that was not his business anyway! Then I produced my resident's card and he asked to see my passport. I trembled, for my old passport had been lost and my new one had not got a Portuguese stamp on it. I do not know whether the Lord blinded his eyes or not, but he looked over the pages and told me to go right ahead. Without a pass! I thanked him and backed my way out, bowing the best bow I had ever made! I went up the road with a Hallelujah, just praising the Lord.

There was a car waiting that very morning, as it were for

me, and I reached Bissau quite late that Friday night. When the Lord is in a thing, my, doesn't it go?

And how did it go for Bessie, now back in her beloved Bissau and reunited with her spiritual children? On her very first day in the city she met 'by accident' the Chief Civil Administrator who was more than a little surprised to see her! On his advice she went at once to arrange an interview with the Governor. That was fixed for the Monday afternoon. On Sunday she gathered with her 'family' in the home of a Christian tailor, in the room which had been their meeting-place ever since officialdom had barred the door of their rented premises.

The house, though poor, was all arranged for the meeting. A clean white cloth was on the table, and there were three pots of flowers in the middle. Bibles and hymn-books were scattered around. Over twenty folks gathered. Oh my, what joy! You can't imagine it! Each Christian gave testimony. Mimi, the only woman convert, brought four or five others. Two were converted a few days later. Some have waited three years or more for my return in order to confess their faith in Christ, thinking that they couldn't do it without me!

That first weekend back in Bissau was more than memorable. Just as Bessie was arranging an interview with the Governor, the Roman Catholic Bishop, whose opposition could have influenced any decision, was preparing to sail off on holiday. His ship pulled out of port on Sunday.

On Monday the entire group of believers fasted and prayed until the matter of the visas should be settled. Again feeling that she was re-enacting the role of Queen Esther, Bessie presented herself before the Governor. Little did she know that the Governor who had been in office when she left and who had very emphatically declared that she would never set foot again in Portuguese Guinea, had just been replaced by one more tolerant. God had timed her visit. His Excellency received her with great kindness, promising to deal with the business of the visas with the utmost expediency. Her courage strengthened by kindness, Bessie had the audacity to ask permission to remain in Bissau without a visa until the reply should come from Lisbon. He was somewhat taken aback, but politely acceded to her irregular request. That part of the battle was over. Surely now victory was just ahead. Bessie rushed off to share the news.

That evening another three were added to the group of Christians. There was such rejoicing, such wonderful times of Bible study and prayer. As Barros, the tall young man who had cried unashamedly when Bessie had left, said, "Miss Bessie, now we are comforted. Our Pastora has returned."

But the war entered a new phase—another period of waiting.

The time dragged on. The weeks passed, and no answer. I felt I simply had to do something. Here were the rains coming. My husband and my baby were over the border in another country. Soon the roads would be impassable. I had a terrible yearning to go back to them. I would pace up and down the hotel room where I was staying, praying and pleading with God for an answer. I went back to the Governor and he promised to send a telegram right away to Lisbon. I got the help of the British Consul who also sent a telegram. I got the Bank Manager to put in a word on my behalf. I did everything possible to get these visas. I had other tests. Money from the bank in Dakar had been frozen, and instead of getting the £20 which Leslie had transferred I got £2. Then the Lord sent a group of American missionaries through this way. I helped them as they did not have the language. In appreciation they left a love-gift which covered my hotel expenses. Besides, I had helped out the proprietor with the use of my camp-beds, so that reduced my bill too.

One day I went out to lunch with a French friend. She lived at the top of quite a high building. While I was sitting there the telegram boy, one of our Christians, came in and discreetly pushed a scrappy piece of paper into my hand. I read the words, "Authorisation for three British subjects to enter Portuguese Guinea." I couldn't say a word or I'd have gotten him the sack. I couldn't even squeak a Hallelujah! I just had to wait to be officially called.

While she waited in faith and impatience, two of the converts came to her at different times saying that God had spoken to them through dreams with the assurance that prayer for the visas had been answered. But a five-day silence was imposed on her before she received Government information of the granting of the visas.

I had told Leslie in Senegal that if I came back on a big truck, he would know that we were all going down, bag and baggage, to Portuguese Guinea. I left Bissau at five o'clock one morning and went right the whole way up to Kounkanne on a hired truck. When we got near to the station, I said to the driver, "You sound on that horn. Make it good and loud. Don't stop. This is a day of victory. The Lord has wonderfully undertaken for us."

But we must go back a bit, to Leslie and Norman and the Barrons in Kounkanne and see how they fared while Bessie was in Bissau. Leslie reported:

We in Senegal fought the fight of faith. Every night Norman prayed, "Please Jesus, send Mummy back with the choos (shoes), wooties (sweeties) and the wisas (visas) and let her bring a big motor-car to take us back to Bissau." And every car that entered the village, he pricked up his ears and said, "Dat Mummy?" Through an article in our W.E.C. magazine, I was led to claim victory with the authority given to us by Jesus. So we began to pack until the verandah was lined with screwed-down boxes, and our ears were strained night and day listening for the purring of an engine on the Pirada road. First a letter came saying that the visas were not yet through but that they in Bissau were strong in faith and would turn up with a lorry just as soon as the visas came. The letter also said that houses were impossible to get. One couple, Government employees, had waited eighteen months, living in a hotel at prices we could never afford. Well, we prayed and the Lord said, "Knock and it shall be opened unto you." Forty days went by—the Bible period of testing—our faith trembling and wobbling but not altogether taking flight.

On the forty-first day we heard it, gradually growing louder until all the compound was in a ferment. Then we saw the lorry turn our way. Yes, it must be. It was. The lorry turned in at the drive, and we were all talking together. "We have the visas! We've got a house! We must leave tomorrow at dawn!"

Next morning early we were off on the last lap of our journey from England to Bissau. Torrents of rain could not dampen our spirits, nor could the sticking in the mud nor the weariness of the long miles with our little fellow on our knees. As we crossed the frontier our hearts gave one great leap. At last we were in 'the Promised Land'. Next day at midday we drove into Bissau. Two days later we were moving into our own house, ideal for a mission headquarters, chosen of God. A week later, we had fifty people inside and a huge crowd outside in the street for the dedication service. When God's time comes, nothing can stop His will being done.

A piece of paper, carefully treasured over the years, witnesses to faith triumphant, for on it during Bessie's absence, Leslie had scribbled the words, "I believe God will give us the visas and the house. We will open up Bissau, Bolama, the Bijagos Islands and Balanta country." This was his declaration. Now the first door had swung wide. In God's time there was to be a fulfilment of the vision.

IO

"THE TREASURED HARVEST of West Africa is not its oil-palm forests nor its golden crop of rice, not even its acres and acres of yellow-flowered peanut plants, but its masses of sons and daughters. Of these there are half a million to be found in Portuguese Guinea."

Sons and daughters—a family relationship, where love, giving and sharing are all a part, where there are bound to be problems, where some grow and mature more quickly than others, where differences of abilities have to be integrated to achieve maximum potential—this is what the missionaries work for under God. From the rapidly growing company of believers in Bissau, a young man was appointed to head up a campaign for the spread of literature, Sunday School superintendents were chosen, a music leader and treasurer emerged and one with the gifts of an evangelist was training. Besides, the Church was early taught to fast and to tithe, the proceeds going towards church extension. Together the Christians decided on a name for the work, calling it 'The Evangelical Church of Portuguese Guinea'.

For the first months Leslie was limited in his use of the language, so that the burden of the preaching fell on Bessie. But Leslie put a great deal into the preparation of themes especially for the instruction classes. He would work out a series, for example, 'The Apostles' Creed', and prepare flannelgraph illustrations for the benefit of those who found personal study difficult or impossible.

Those were halcyon days in the work when the grace of God was evident, when the number of believers increased steadily and the Church grew and flourished. How true it has ever been that where there is simplicity, poverty, even lack of material possessions and educational facilities, there the grace of God has more scope, the activity of God is more clearly seen and so He is glorified.

The evening meeting was in progress when a strange-looking man was seen peering in at the window. He seemed somewhat drunk and the blotchy skin-pigmentation of his face gave him a hideous appearance. When he walked into the room Bessie was rather scared, until he spoke his name and said he wanted to be converted. Victor M. had come from the Cubiseque area, from the town of Impada, to answer in a court case for charges brought against him. Life at that moment for him seemed to be one load of trouble within and without and hardly worth hanging on to. There was little possibility of his being acquitted, he thought. In this mood he had been walking in the Bissau park when a believer prayerfully handed him a tract. At that critical point in his life, a tiny glimmer of hope penetrated his gloom. He determined to search out the meeting place for he was already convinced that this Jesus of the tract had to give what he most needed. That night, fumbling for words so little did he know, he made his first most urgent prayer. In answer God not only gave him liberty from himself and sin, but public exoneration from the charges made against him. He began to learn the promptings of the Spirit, and to obey. One night after his conversion, he visited his usual tavern for a drink, but as he put the glass to his lips, a feeling of nausea swept through him so that he could not touch it. Thinking that a smoke might help matters he lit up a cigarette but one drag made him feel worse. He recognised the voice of God and broke with the habits, never to touch them again. From then on he became a most ardent Bible student, and, before he returned to his own area in the south as an ordained evangelist, he had already given over his house in one of the suburbs of Bissau to the preaching of the Gospel. Then he was off to spread the Good News in the Impada area, witnessing, trekking, proving the power of God in healing, preparing the way for the missionaries to visit later on.

Mimi too, the first woman convert, left Bissau and went off to the Bijagos Islands, the home of twenty-five thousand of Guinea's most primitive people. The journey was 'for her health's sake'. How wonderfully God plans it all out. She was one who just could not keep quiet. She knew the Lord in a very deep way, loved His Word and had led several to Him in Bissau. Now she was to be the pioneer to the Bijagos. It was an added miracle when she was able to rent a six-roomed house, ample accommodation for the missionary family as soon as that would be needed.

That first Christmas, it was decided to put on a special programme, a precedent that has been followed over the years. The theme chosen was, 'Christ, the Light of the World'. It took days of trial and error of materials, and hours of labour and frustration before Bessie and Leslie succeeded in constructing a lighthouse in eight sections, each of which represented one aspect of the character of the Lord Jesus. Then came the teaching of their parts to the believers.

"Practice nights revealed tremendous unpreparedness. One poor lad read his piece as if he were reciting the alphabet. Another shouted at the top of his voice like an open-air salesman."

Christmas Eve came. An expectant crowd jammed the little room and packed the pavement outside. Those taking part rose to the occasion. As the sections were put in position, the initial letters spelt out the word Emmanuel. The lights were dimmed while another light shone out brightly from the top of the model, representing the Light of the World.

On the following morning, a Service of Adoration of the Lord Jesus was arranged. In Leslie's words:

The Church was nicely prepared and looked peaceful, but we had no flowers. The Lord put it into the heart of a friend to send a lovely bunch of red roses just before the service began. Only half a dozen people arrived on time, but others followed them, and still others, until I had to sit in the porch. We finished up with more than we usually get to a Sunday morning service. The Lord gave us a quiet time of meeting with Himself, which was the highlight of the festive season for me—for is not the objective of missionary work to see those who were in darkness transformed and able to praise the Saviour from overflowing hearts? There they were, those who before Bessie's advent in 1941 were ignorant of salvation, now praising God for Christmas, for a Saviour, for light and liberty in the Holy Ghost. Just as various types met at the manger to adore, so here, in our little gathering were high and low, black and white, educated and illiterate. God had been born in their hearts and we met to adore and offer our gifts. Such is the joy of missionary work—a joy which cannot be excelled.

'Bissau . . . Bolama.' God had surely spoken the word, and so the fire burned within to burst into flame when Bessie, Leslie and Norman called in there on their return from a trip to the Bijagos Islands and Mimi. The town had already been well covered with Christian literature during Bessie's absence, but when the boat pulled in at the harbour there was no one there to meet the family as they had not been able to advise any of the friends of their coming. The devil had fought every inch of the way to wreck this trip. There had been sickness, Church problems and transport difficulties. Now they were glad to get ashore for Norman's temperature was high. Malaria was on the way. The news of their arrival shot through the town in no time at all. Before long a small two-roomed, flag-floored Cape Verdian house had been rented where for one week they held preaching meetings every evening.

The 2nd of February, the fourth anniversary of our wedding, and Bessie's birthday were approaching, but there was little hope of buying presents here to celebrate. Would not the Lord Himself provide? Bessie preached that night in spite of an inflamed throat. At the end of the evening everybody wanted to be converted! Dubious about the reality of their desires, we made it easier for them to go away after the meeting than to stay. They ALL stayed! Bessie said to me at supper afterwards, "There is your anniversary present." I had to ask her not to go so fast for I myself had asked the Lord for that present for HER! So the Bolama Church was born.

One of the first converts was a man known for his violent behaviour, his frequent drunkenness and his wild brawls. He would go into the tavern and with a sweep of his hand smash every glass within reach, cursing and swearing and making a nuisance of himself. But God met with him in such a way that he was unrecognisable as the same person in his new life. Gone were the oaths, the abusiveness, the rage and the tempers. In their place was a quiet reverent spirit. A new-made person, he learned the way of prayer and faith and was known for the meekness of his character.

As in Bissau, conditions in Bolama were quite primitive at first in the meeting room—packing cases, rug-covered trunks, borrowed stools and chairs. One of the neighbours, who had not dared to come into any of the meetings, was persuaded one evening to lend all his chairs and so he had to join with the company in order to sit down! That night he too became a Christian.

The birth of a Church—what a moment of exquisite joy!

How aptly it is likened to its physical counterpart. The exhausting struggle is over—there is life. Then follow the long months and even years of patient caring, days and nights of watching, praying, trusting, until the age of responsible maturity is reached. So it was in Bolama. Spiritual life had begun. Later on, Bessie and Leslie were to spend much time in bringing up this their second spiritual baby.

Just before the rains set in in May 1946 a visit to Impada was arranged. Victor M. had returned to Bissau with the thrilling news of the way the work was going in his area. He very much wanted the missionaries to come and see for themselves. So they set out again, first by boat to Bolama, where Bessie and Norman stopped off, and then by canoe to Impada.

All went well for a couple of minutes (wrote Leslie) as the oarsmen pulled away from the shore. Then the master of the canoe shouted over that the price would be more than that agreed. No, we would not pay as much, so back we rowed to the land, and deadlock ensued for a time. At last a compromise was reached—he would accept the original price, but before we set out on the journey to ensure that he got it. Lap, lap, lap again went the oars into the glass-like waters of Bolama Bay. All went well until we reached Colonia, a wild, rocky promontory down the canal. Mutiny suddenly developed among the crew. For hours the little boat just drifted around, two of the oarsmen sitting back making no effort to right the canoe on its course. Tides played havoc with us at their will and the canoe drifted backwards, so Victor ordered them to put us ashore until they settled their differences. At last they got through and we were under way again but valuable time had been irrevocably lost. To avoid spending the night on the water, we asked that we might be put to land at a spot just halfway to our destination. As this was the end of the motor road, we were able to walk the remaining distance, some eighteen miles, by stages. After a night at a friend's house and other stops along the way to sell Bibles and gossip the Gospel, we finally began the last stage of the march at dawn the following day. Time stands still here in Africa, but it seems even to go backwards in Cubiseque. Rain-clouds were now threatening and soon the storm broke, heavily at first and then just a steady, soaking fall. The sky was as black as ink and the way unknown—to me. On and on we stumbled until at last the flickering oil lamps of the houses of Impada came into sight. Too late to make food for that night, we rolled into bed after the welcomes were over, and forgot till morning.

They were startled into life again by early morning visitors, curious to have a look at the first white missionary ever to set foot in those parts. Later on in the week it was their joy to help four of them into believing in Jesus. The first was a Bijagos boy whose keenness showed from the start and whose life they at once coveted for the Lord. He was later to become Head Student at the Bible School and an evangelist.

Yet another spiritual birth had taken place, another infant Church, very tiny in its inception, had been produced. While the work was still in its initial stages, an urgent appeal was made for the 'pastora' to visit them. When that became possible, their greatest joy was to see some of the wives of the Christian men enter into the way of faith in Jesus. It has been the custom from time immemorial for these people to live in concubinage. Victor had his share of problems along this line too. The whole situation required most careful handling. Bessie took on the job of instructing the women while Leslie dealt with the men. Some had never thought of legalising their marriage. Their whole background and way of thinking did not lead them to consider it worthwhile, nor did the example of Europeans in the Colony help them to regard it as desirable. But when one woman came saying she wanted to become a Christian, Bessie recognised her as one of Victor's concubines.

Two had already left him many years previously, and this was no break in custom. Now he had a wife and this concubine. When she spoke her name, Bessie looked at her steadily asking her if she really did want to get right with God. Yes, she did. Was she willing then to turn her back on her old life of sin, to turn from Victor and living with him? Again she said she was. At that point Victor and Leslie were called in.

I shall never forget it. There sat Victor and Jennie who had had children by him and who for eight years had been his concubine. Victor said, "I have nothing against you, but we have been living in the devil's way. Now I am determined to go God's way. You want to go God's way too, so we shall part. If ever you are hungry, I will give you bread to eat. You will never starve nor be in need, but we cannot go on with that life any longer." I had such a lump in my throat I could hardly swallow. But God delivered that man and his concubine.

Sons and daughters—in Bissau, Bolama, Impada—young Churches struggling for their very existence, learning the processes of growing up in the Spirit, spiritual leaders emerging from each group, teachers, evangelists and pastors being anointed of God for their ministry, a re-enactment of the history of every Church since Pentecost—the vision was taking shape. The declaration of faith on the scrappy piece of paper was becoming reality. It was all God's doing, and it was truly wonderful.

II

"The people who were dwelling in darkness have now seen a great light; those who were living in the land of shadows, upon them the light has shone."

"Darkness . . . the land of shadows" could well describe Balanta country as Bessie and Leslie found it on their first trip there in 1946. In the villages there were fetishes everywhere—a few sticks in the ground as a marriage fetish, a rack of animal skulls and jawbones in every home where offerings are made when the Baltana wishes to consult the spirits of his ancestors, fetishes to guard the room, the individual and the village, and all of these demanding honour and sacrifice. Everywhere too there was an abundance of uncleanliness. Pigs sniffled and snorted amongst the piles of refuse in the middle of the compounds. Flies swarmed in profusion and landed germ-laden and without discrimination on human and animal flesh. Scraggy hens picked up what scraps they could, while pot-bellied babies, their eyes inflamed and running, sat on the sand. Clothing was of the scantiest, a dirty loincloth or even just a tortoise shell. Such poverty, such dirt, such darkness: it could be felt.

Bissora is the administrative centre of this Balanta area. It is a town boasting of a few shops whose main trade seems to be liquor and tobacco. From the town, like the spokes of a wheel, many paths leading to the tribal villages radiate. Such need was apparent in all of this district. How was it to be met? God has His own marvellous ways. He provided accommodation in a native house in the town as a starting point. From there the Light began to penetrate first of all into the hearts of the 'civilised' population of the town. They formed the nucleus of the first Balanta Church. Then to this young Church God sent Edmundo, a young man of Balanta origin and language, who had found Christ while living in Bissau. He had served with the missionaries and for two years had trained as an evangelist under their leadership. His commission was to pastor the Church and to concentrate evangelism in the villages. He laid his plans very methodically and set to work opening up half a dozen villages right away to the Gospel.

We visited them all and were thrilled. Here is Chief Malan's village. Our first impression as we step through the enclosure is of a huge mound of cow-dung. They keep the cows in the enclosure in the middle of the huts and never sweep up. You can imagine the rest! Over there is a hut curiously painted in red with pillars holding up the roof. It is the boys' hut, for they all live together. Further round the circle is an old dilapidated hut belonging to the father of the Chief, and next to that is the Chief's hut. In we go to greet him. While I sit and chat with him, Edmundo goes after his congregation. Soon the youngsters arrive, each on the back of a cow, for the herdboys get quite adept at riding the cows about the place. Then come the older lads. They make a fine group as Edmundo gathers them together for their meeting. They start off with a chorus or two which Edmundo has translated into Balanta. There follows a Bible reading in Portuguese with an explanation in Baltana, then a sermon lasting for forty-five minutes! Such attention! Such quietness! I sit amazed.

There we must leave Edmundo, as the Brierleys did, on his

own among his own people, for urgent business and the need of the Bissau Church called them back to the city.

It is not surprising to find that as the city Church grew and became effective opposition came from various quarters. The Christians were taunted and persecuted by their mates at work and their relatives at home. The Roman Catholics did their utmost to hinder the work. There was uproar in the city on the day when some Catholic nursing-sisters allowed a cartoon of the Protestant Church to be pinned up on the wall of the out-patient department of the hospital. Bessie was there playing the organ. Others easily recognisable were caricatured around her. Others were relegated to the trees around and portrayed as monkeys. No one, of course, was responsible! The doctor in charge ordered it to be taken down.

The matter of Church development soon became an urgent item of business when the elders got together. Should they continue with one focal point for meetings at the centre of the city? Should they not rather formulate a plan for reaching into the suburbs? It was then that the vision was given of obtaining rooms in each of the language quarters of the town. These would be used as preaching-halls. This was an entirely legal procedure, whereas preaching in the street was forbidden. These suburban meetings were signally blessed of God in the addition of new Christians. In this way the work of God advanced amongst the poorer classes of the city, the less privileged, the less literate, the tribespeople who form their particular agglomerations. Every preaching hall became a birthplace, and every soul won for Christ a demonstration of the power of God.

The meetings which had begun in one of the rooms of the missionary house had overgrown the allotted space until two rooms were in almost constant use as Church premises and the family had to squeeze itself into the remaining one. By now Norman was a growing youngster, and their cramped quarters gave them little place for quiet preparation and study. Search was made for a more suitable building for the Church, but there was nothing available. The only solution seemed to be that the family should move out to allow the Church in the city to develop its corporate life and witness. The thought of leaving her much-loved and memory-filled home was not an easy one for Bessie. Her life was people—people to whom she could talk, people whom she could help. A move out to the suburbs would change all that, or so she imagined! Out there, people were in tribal groups, and communication would be much more difficult. Eventually a native house in much need of repair and going at a ridiculously low price was found for them. It was right on the edge of the city amongst the Papel people. As with some heartache and not a few tears she packed her few belongings and the mostly African-made furniture and made the move out to Bissau Novo, who could have foreseen then that that scarcely habitable house was to become in the course of time a mission headquarters, a centre of witness, Church premises, Bible school, medical centre and childrens' home in turn?

The opening up of Bissau Novo station partly solved another growing problem. The city Church in its development had included all types of converts, but it soon became evident that the illiterate servant boys could not assimilate teaching as easily as the educated Portuguese-speaking civil servants. There was no discrimination for all were equally loved. But it was more profitable for all that instruction should be given in Portuguese to those who could understand, and in Creole, a 'pidgin' form of the language, to the others. In this way it was decided to split the city Church, the educated believers attending the original place of worship, and the others forming a second group in Bissau Novo. This gave opportunity for further expansion. Indeed a whole new area around Bissau Novo began to open up.

A church building was designed and erected at the back of the mission house. Here school was commenced for those who could as yet not read. Boys from the nearby villages joined in, and the first convert in that area was a Papel schoolboy from a village just down the road. Within a week twelve others followed, their ages varying from adolescence to middle age. It was not too long before an indigenous Church, which was latterly to become Bessie's 'crown and joy', came into being. It appointed its elders and deacons, each one of them a fetishist before conversion, under the fear of witchcraft and the power of the evil one. How mightily God delivered!

Joaquim was a quiet type, a stonemason. When he began to frequent the meetings, Amelia, his Papel wife, prepared her things and was ready for off. She did not want a husband who despised the fetish, she insisted. Joaquim resorted to prayer, asking the Lord to prevent his wife leaving the home for he loved her, and life without her would be impossible. Amelia stayed. Not only so, she began coming to the weekly women's meetings which Bessie conducted in the mission house. In time she gave herself to the Lord, and from then she could not be restrained—speaking of what God had done for her, visiting the homes of her friends, urging them to get right with God. The women confided in her instead of running off to the witch-doctor. Many times she prayed for healing for her neighbours' children. Life for both Joaquim and Amelia became so different. Soon the desire came to them to enrol for Bible School, but Amelia could neither read nor write, a very obvious difficulty. Still, she would not be put off. So it was agreed that they should start Bible training the following year in the Bible School that was still to be built. Suddenly, when life held every prospect, Amelia was taken to hospital where she gave birth to twins. Within a few hours she passed into the presence of the Lord. Joaquim had time just to get into the hospital and lovingly commit her to Him before she went away. It seemed to him as if the bottom had dropped out of his world. The one on whom he leaned had been taken from him, and in her place were two tiny helpless babes, Benjamin and Lydia. To hand them over to Amelia's relations would have meant their being brought up as fetishists. To leave them in the hospital would have meant their eventual removal to the Catholic orphanage. There was only one answer—Bessie must take them. Such a handful all of a sudden, but she loved those babes, as if they were her very own.

Then there were the women of the suburbs. They were so obdurate, so conniving, so bound by fetish fear, that Bessie wondered many times if ever there would be any response from amongst them. The Christian men who were already married before conversion had a very hard time, especially if they had children, for the mothers would refuse to bring them for any medical help, demanding money from their husbands to go to the witch-doctor. Sometimes, after long and weary struggles, the husband would have to allow his wife to leave him, while he was left in an unenviable situation in a heathen culture. Instruction was regularly given about Christian marriage and prayer was often made about the marital situation, but there seemed such little hope. But God . . . The arrival of trained personnel made the medical work more effective. The Spirit of God broke through the darkness and superstition as the Word was preached at the women's meetings. One after another these pagan, illiterate, fear-bound women sought salvation and experienced the enlightening and liberating power of the Gospel. What joy, at last, to be able to celebrate a Christian wedding in the Bissau Novo church. Bessie loved such occasions when she was 'mother' to all the brides. The first one was Jenny who married Adolpho. What a lovely bride she made in her blue dress, and flowers in her hair. It was easy to guess who had arranged them. This was a landmark in the national church history and gave courage to some of the more timid ones who eventually sought to solemnise their marriages in the Christian way. Through these unions the Church was strengthened, Christian families were brought into being and Christian homes became centres of witness throughout the neighbourhood.

No matter how willing, two people alone cannot take all the burden of such a rapidly growing work. Not that Bessie and Leslie did not want to share it, but reinforcements were not being allowed to enter the country. For a very long time the door seemed tightly shut until almost imperceptibly a little chink of light shone through. Then slowly and noiselessly the door began to swing open.

The story of the founding of the Leper and Medical Crusade is told elsewhere.* It is the story of one woman's triumph of faith when everything was against her. Edith Moules was a missionary under W.E.C. in Congo when God gave her the vision of a great leprosy-treatment programme not only for Congo but for the already existing W.E.C. fields of West Africa. There followed the greatest test of all. Her beloved husband, Percy, died very suddenly, and she was left to see the project through on her own. Added to this was her rapidly deteriorating health. When she visited Portuguese Guinea in 1947, she already had well-founded suspicions that she was the victim of cancer. But that did not deter her from her planned itinerary of the fields.

For Mrs. Moules ('Ma Moli') Bessie had the greatest esteem. She recalled Ma Moli's earlier visits to Arthur's Mission and the influence they had had on her. Now, when she visited Portuguese Guinea, the two women spent long and profitable hours together. Although Bessie was not medically trained she was most enthusiastic about the possibilities of a Leprosy-Medical work. Accordingly an interview with the Governor was requested for Ma Moli and was granted.

"Mrs. Moules was able to put before him our scheme for collaboration with the various Governments and to give him some idea of what had been accomplished in Congo. He sat entranced listening to the details. He offered to help us in any way possible, asking us to submit an official request in writing.

*Who Is My Neighbour? by Edith Moules (Christian Literature Crusade)

This has been done and to our amazement a favourable reply has been received from the Central Government in Lisbon."

The reply agreed to the establishment of a leprosarium and the admission into the Colony of specialised personnel of British or American origin. The door had swung wide open. The first three to step over the threshold were American girls—Ruth Bergh, Marie Bakken and Valborg Esping. Now instead of two missionaries trying desperately to extend themselves over three main stations, they were five. It seemed such a crowd!

By now, as a result of persistent praying and faithful giving friends at home had raised enough to enable Bessie and Leslie to buy a car. What a help that was to them in their frequent journeys, even though Bessie's nerves were strained on the pot-holed roads and the narrow, twisting tracks. There was one part of journeying which really scared her—ferry crossings—and there seemed to be no end of them on the many inland water-ways of Guinea. Leslie would stop the car to allow Bessie and Norman to get out. Then she would tense up, shut her eyes and clench her fists while Leslie drove at snail pace on to the plat-form of the canoe or log-ferry, taking care not to overshoot at the far end. Then, when the sound of the engine cut out she would look and relax. All was safe. She would climb aboard and chatter away to the oarsmen. But she hated those cross-ings.

By November 1949 an American doctor, Herbert Billman, and the first trained nurse from England had arrived. In a small mud and thatched building erected on the mission concession in Bissora, a clinic for leprosy treatment was set up with the doctor in charge. How unpretentious it all was, but opportunity had been grasped by faith, an opportunity which was multi-plied and proved effective not only in the number of clinics opened but in the number of Churches established through this means.

Bessie and Leslie were now in their sixth year of service.

Norman had already started schooling, and with a Dad and Mum who were so often on the move, that proved quite a problem. Education took place at convenient moments and had to be omitted when there were no convenient moments. It was a great relief to the family when Ruth Bergh took over the daily lessons.

The first sheaves of the 'treasured harvest' had been carefully and joyfully gathered in. Two Churches had been formed in Bissau, elders had been ordained and the suburbs were being evangelised. Bolama, too, had yielded its first sheaves. When God gave a larger house there instead of the small rented room an attempt was made at starting a Bible School. This was a temporary measure as the building of a permanent School in the Bissora area was in progress. At Impada the Church met under the pastoral care of Victor and it showed signs of growth. Belonging to this Church were the first Bijagos converts, those who had come over from the Archipelago to earn a living. Balanta country was being opened up by Edmundo the evangelist while Doc Billman was finding his way in the intricacies of language-learning and tropical medicine.

It was time now for a well-earned furlough. There was so much still to accomplish—the leprosy programme, the Bible School project, the evangelisation of the Bijagos Archipelago, the tackling of African languages—as well as the daily burden of the Churches. But they must have a break. Others could carry on in their absence. They would return as quickly as possible.

12

"A WOMAN WHO fears the Lord is to be praised."

By the end of 1951 Miss Bessie, as she was still so affectionately called, was back amongst her own people for the third term of service. In the few spare moments which she had during the first months after her return, family affairs claimed priority. There was the matter of Norman's education in a school for missionaries' children at Mamou, across the frontier in French Guinea. Kind friends at home had offered to pay all the expenses incurred. Then there was another little Brierley on the way, due, if reckoning were right, at the end of February. With what joy Bessie anticipated this event. Several friends were sewing garments, a pram had been given and a cot promised. When it was all over, the family planned to take Norman to school and return to Bissau just before Easter.

It was almost mid-day with the sun hotter than usual for January when a young cripple lad, a Christian from the village at the back of the mission house, came hobbling up to the door. In great distress he pleaded with Bessie to come to the help of his sister who had been in labour the whole night through. But how could she? She was in no condition to do so, her ankles were swollen and she needed to rest in the heat of the day. Besides she was not a midwife, and the mission midwife was in town. The lad turned away sadly. As he did so, Bessie's heart smote her. Would she not have appreciated help in such circumstances? She could not efface the disappointed look of the lad from her mind. She hurried indoors, packed a shopping bag with a few things she thought might be useful and was off in haste after the boy.

She found the sister under a tree, exposed to dirt, heat and flies, and crying in agony. With help she lifted the lass into a hut. Then, kneeling on the rough floor beside her she prayed for help. An enema might be the answer, she thought. She sent someone off to warm up some water. Then prayer, faith and works combined with the result that in no time at all a baby boy was born.

"I washed the baby's eyes, prayed and gave thanks to the Lord. It did me good to see the good hand of the Lord even upon these poor ignorant folks. They came the other day to the house and asked me to write down the baby's date of birth and to give him a name, so I called him Joao (John)."

By now the date on the calendar showed that either there had been a miscalculation or that her babe was overdue. Anxious days followed when Bessie got exceedingly weary, until at the end of March a little boy, Ernest, was born—to live for only seventeen short hours, just long enough for Bessie to cradle him in her arms in motherly love.

"He was a fine little chap," Leslie wrote home, "and we'd have liked to keep him longer, but the Lord took him to Himself . . . we'll meet him some day and enjoy that which we have not been permitted to enjoy down here."

Meanwhile the doctor rushed around to save Bessie's life. A severe haemorrhage necessitated an immediate blood transfusion. She was transferred to hospital and later, to her unceasing delight, she discovered that she had been given a transfusion of Balanta blood.

The wound caused by the loss of her babe ran deep, the pain searing for many days and when it healed the scar remained tender. For weeks Bessie struggled to find peace of heart and the assurance that no avoidable mistake had been made. Hot uncomfortable days and restless nights set her mind off on a succession of unanswerable questions which led always to the same conclusion—"with God there are no second causes"—a phrase which she repeated again and again, till at last she accepted her loss and made ready to face her next family event, that of getting Norman to school.

"Norman is looking forward to going to school. I think that will be another great pull at the heart-strings for me, but the Lord will give grace I'm sure. He gave his heart to the Lord on New Year's eve."

So they set out for French Guinea and Mamou only to run into trouble after trouble with the car until they had eventually to abandon the project and limp back into Bissau for repairs.

Norman was of course disappointed, for we had gone two hundred miles of the way when the car failed, and so we had to return. Now we are linked up with the Parent Union School, and poor Norman goes through his paces with his Daddy most days. It isn't exactly fun to live in a country where they talk in escudos, kilometres and kilograms, and have school books which teach pounds, shillings and pence, ounces and miles. When you buy four ounces of sweets at so many shillings a pound, the answer is apt to come in escudos! Then up comes King Alfred, the Celts and the ancient Britons, and here he is surrounded by Papels shouting around outside while doing their initiation rites. In nature lessons they talk of robin redbreast, the wild rose and the oak, while there isn't a sight of one in a thousand miles.

That disappointment, however, was clearly of God's appointing, for as one of the other missionaries who was involved in helping with Norman's lessons wrote, "Bessie needed that boy. Most of us think that it is our children that need us, but maybe sometimes it is the other way round. Of course, that loving, sensitive boy needed his mother too for a few more years."

The third term of service saw considerable increase in the number of missionaries, both from Britain and the United States. With the opening up of leprosy treatment clinics, permission had been granted by the Government for the entry of further personnel, provided they were involved in this work. To every new missionary Bessie was more than a mother, helping them through their sticky patches, advising them on their conduct towards those whom they had come to serve, insisting on a sensible attitude to food—"better to spend a bit extra on a good meal than a whole lot on medicine"—a reasonable amount of rest and a disciplined programme of work. For every newcomer there was a welcoming party. Indeed, parties were one of Bessie's specialities. She loved to entertain. She had the ability, probably inherited from her mother, of making a little go a long way. As long as eggs and flour were available, she would concoct a cake and the most plain-looking affair would be titivated into looking something special. Not that Bessie ever spent a great deal of time on trivialities for everything was done with typical whirlwind vivacity, yet the effect was that everyone felt honoured and, for the occasion at least, a Very Important Person. New recruits coming out from their home bases with preconceived ideas of missionary living were often taken by surprise to find a lace tablecloth and dainty china, brought out for the event. They soon learned that a silver tea-service and a few flowers—how Bessie loved flowers—had an uplifting effect on one's morale. Even on trek in the most 'bush' environment, when tin trunks and boxes served as tables and chairs, there was always a tablecloth of sorts, if only a clean towel or a calico sugar-bag.

We had done a day's travelling together, two missionary families, surveying and bookselling. When daylight had almost gone we visited the home of the nearest Administrator hoping for overnight lodgings, only to be told that there was accommodation at a village 'not too far away' in the Government rest-house. The rest-house turned out to be a two-roomed, empty, doorless building into which the goats and pigs wandered at will. Disconsolately we looked into the place comparing it with the luxury we had just left. Then, making a joke of our mod. cons., we laughed uproariously, which had the salutory effect of setting us to work with a will. We made switches of dried grass and chased the animals and the dirt out of the way. Before darkness closed in on us Bessie's expertise with on-the-spot drapes and decorations had transformed the shanty into a reasonable dwelling. She had found some wild flowers, and a used food-can did the rest. Indeed we were almost sorry to leave our temporary home, staying an extra night in it before moving on to a still more empty barn.

Portuguese Guinea and the birth of the National Church had been in a particular way Bessie's baby. She loved every Christian dearly, but not jealously. When eventually the time came to share responsibility with other missionaries, she did so gladly, and still found her hands full. But what of these new helpers? One of them tells us.

It must have been disconcerting for the Brierleys to find us unprepared in so many ways. The three of us had reached the thirty mark, yet when we were asked to preach a sermon, it was rather obvious that we were just not accustomed to doing this kind of thing. None of us could play a musical instrument. The Brierleys had waited too long for help, however, to be discouraged by what we could NOT do. They often said that they were glad that we knew how to pray. As more missionaries came, so there were those inevitable rubs that come when people live in close community. At such times Bessie would say, "All of you have the love of God in your hearts and a living faith in the Lord Jesus. That is certain or you would not be here. So we'll just begin from that point."

From the point of love to the Lord—that must surely be the basis of every relationship as yet another missionary was to prove. She was smarting somewhat from the scolding she had received from Bessie and was feeling a bit resentful. But then she had been foolish enough to neglect the advice which had so often been given to her. While she was inwardly hurt she kept away, until she fell ill. It seemed then that the devil was going to score a victory by getting her off the field. But no. Bessie and Leslie stood by her, took her into their personal care, nursed her, prayed for her, refusing to give up until she was completely recovered. Strict and straight to the point Bessie could be, but she never held a grudge.

"People of the world don't know how to forgive," she would say. "But I pray that God will give me always a forgiving spirit and a good forgettery. Too many of us say we forgive, but we don't know how to forget."

Love to her Lord—it motivated so much that was Bessie. When the time came for the first missionary wedding on the field, it was Bessie who dug into her trunks to unearth a length of precious white satin to make a bridal gown. When supplies ran short at a certain church 'festa', it was Bessie who robbed her garden of pumpkins to feed the crowd. When a friend was going home to Portugal, it was Bessie's winter coat and gloves that were brought out from their wrappings and went with her to keep her warm. When Amelia, the Christian wife and mother, passed away after giving birth to twins, it was to Bessie's care that the two helpless mites were entrusted.

"She was our mother and our friend," wrote one of the first women converts. Amazingly they looked upon her as such, although she was younger than many of them. Her outgoing personality, her willingness to leave whatever she was engaged in to become involved in their problems, and her immense patience gained their love and confidence. Authority had divided the country into classes—civilised and non-civilised. There were varieties of culture, education and colour, but Bessie was at home with them all. She could as easily sip tea with the ladies of the town and be known for her courtesy and good breeding, as bathe the eyes of a leprosy patient. For, in every situation people knew she loved them.

The young husband of a Cape Verdian family had died quite suddenly. A promising bank clerk, he and his wife had come only spasmodically to Church. But this was their hour of need and Bessie was quick to sense it. Going into that home of mourning and distress, she literally took over, made the funeral arrangements and kept awake all night to give drinks of tea and coffee to the many who visited. Her kindness made a lasting impression not only on the immediate family but on all who came and went.

Dona Juliana, one of the believers rescued from immoral practices, recalls how one night during the rainy season they were having a meeting on the first floor of an old building when a terrific storm blew up. The shattering noise of houses crashing and tumbling around them filled them all with terror. Bessie was leading the meeting, and in a voice loud enough to be heard above the storm, she urged the hundred or so gathered there not to be afraid.

"Jesus is with us," she called out. "He is our Captain. He will keep us safe." Then she began to sing lustily, encouraging them all to join in. Her singing went on above the noise of the storm till fears were stilled. Some wanted to leave, afraid that the floor would collapse and that they would plunge to death, but she insisted that they all stayed until eventually the storm abated at about 2 a.m.

Love demands firmness as Juliana also remembers. After her conversion she gradually learned to live as a Christian in such a way that it made a difference to her home. She swept it clean and made it tidy and she sewed curtains for her windows.

Indeed all was so different that one of her neighbours remarked that it was well worth belonging to the Evangelical Church. But Bessie was disturbed about one thing. Juliana's door was always wide open and she wasted a great deal of time gossiping to all and sundry as they passed by. So Bessie had a movable folding screen made, took it to Juliana's home and placed it in the room by the door so that it afforded her privacy and allowed her to get on with her work while not excluding the air.

Amelia de C. had been converted from a life of demon possession. Her experience was quite remarkable and for some time she made good progress in her Christian faith. Then she allowed herself to be persuaded to attend a tribal dance where the evil spirits were worshipped. This led her into her former troubles. The missionaries, unaware of what had happened, tried to deal with her sympathetically, until one day Bessie found her rolling on the ground and causing a great commotion. With a word of sharp rebuke and with authority she spoke to Amelia, and instantly the woman was delivered.

"Such times are not happy ones in the life of a missionary, but necessary if the world is ever going to be evangelised." Bessie's eyes filled with tears as she wrote the words, and her pen hurried over the letters to be finished. She was back in thought to the moment when she had hugged and hugged her beloved Norman, reluctant to let him go. Then painfully she had walked down the gangplank of the M.V. *Aureol* which was to take him away from her and off to England and to Emmanuel Grammar School, attached to the Swansea Bible College. For two silent hours as the boat slid slowly down the River Gambia into the setting sun and out into the waters of the Atlantic, Bessie and Leslie had stood watching, their hands locked, their hearts too full for words. Now she was reliving it all, remembering that her babe was becoming a man, in possession of his own passport, no longer quite so dependent on her. And she was proud of him! She smiled through her tears as she ended her letter, picturing him already in the classroom amongst the other boys, and knowing deep down that this was the best for him, although it cost her so much.

Babies—it seemed that Bessie's arms were made for them, strong and motherly and tender. The twins were little bundles of fun, occupying much of her time until little Benjamin was taken to see Jesus, and another missionary took charge of Lydia. But then there were other babies to be cared for, little helpless pieces of human stuff whose mothers were leprous patients.

Bessie never forgot the day when a guard in uniform appeared at the door requesting that Mr. Brierley call at once to see the Government leprologist. Opposition to the proposed mission leprosarium had steadily mounted, and the missionaries feared the worst, a shut-down of the whole work. So while Leslie answered the summons, the others got to their knees and pleaded with God for a favourable outcome to the visit. When Leslie returned, Bessie's face showed tenseness as she waited for him to speak. To her unbelieving surprise, Leslie said in quite jovial tones,

"Get your things on, Mummy. We are going to Cumura to fetch a new-born baby."

It transpired that the doctor had asked Leslie if they would be willing to take this child as the Roman Catholic sisters had already taken some others and had no more room. How wonderful God is! He stepped in right at that moment and through the Brierleys' willingness to take a babe, silenced all opposition thus allowing them to carry out their leprosy project for the Colony.

To fetch a new-born babe from a leprous mother in order to care for it seemed such a good idea that Bessie did not ever stop to think that there would be any difficulty. She was to find out differently. That mother loved her little one and hated the thought of parting with her. Why should she give her babe to a white woman anyway? She did not know if she were to be trusted. In a flash Bessie grasped the situation. Had she not known the pain of giving her son into the care of another? She went to the mother and, with all the feeling that her lips and eyes could convey, promised to care for her child. As that African mother slowly relinquished her grasp on her little daughter to hand her over into Bessie's arms, the pain was shared. Little Elizabeth, that first rescued baby, has since grown into a fine young woman.

With the help of Miss Madeleine Rix, Bessie coped with the baby-situation, for from then on, every time a baby was born at the leper settlement of Cumura, Bessie was called to go and fetch it.

"Every so often," she wrote home to those who began to support this work, "the babes are taken up to the settlement to see their mothers. Oh, if you could just see those poor mutilated parents and their delight at seeing their babies! They are not allowed to touch them but the whole population of the camp just crowds around and stares at the little black specks wrapped in their colourful blankets, mostly made by kind hands at home. There are also five Christian young men in the camp, sent there from our Bissora dispensary. They have prayer meetings every day, and when we go up we have a meeting for them."

As the family of babies grew so God provided in wonderful ways. Of course, there were bottle-rounds at regular intervals, piles of daily washing, times of sickness and tummy upsets, nights when sleep was very interrupted. Friends sent clothes from home, not that babes need a great deal of clothing in the heat of the tropics, but money had to be elasticated to pay for the crates of baby foods imported from Europe and U.S.A. Yet, in every time of need there was His provision. In 1955 He sent out a children's nurse, Miss Helen MacKenzie, under whose supervision and love the 'Garden of Happiness' came into being. The testimony of this work of faith undertaken for the children of leprosy patients has still to be written.

One of the desperate needs on the field was for Christian girls as wives for the young men. It was Bessie's idea to take some of them into the various mission homes for training under the instruction of lady missionaries.

If you knew how backward most of them are you would know that our task is no easy one. Our apprentice carpenter asked us to take his future wife into training to see if we could win her for the Lord. Leslie, Michael and a group of our Christian lads went to her village by car to bring her in. When she came out of the forest at the call of her folks she had scarcely a strip of clothing on her and looked such a forlorn little thing. As she was going to the white man's house, her relations thought that clothing was an unnecessary extravagance. She would find plenty there! Leslie made them find a wrap for her before bringing her into Bissau. On her arrival, the boys promptly named her Rebekah, for she had been sent for.

She is now fat and flourishing, learning to sew and to read, clean house and wash. But you can't imagine the headaches one gets during the period of training.

One lad came saying that he had been given a wife by his father, but he did not want to take her until she was a Christian. Would I take her? So she became my third charge . . .

Little Mariazinha is my special care. Her father gave her to me two years ago. I really thought she was hopeless. She kept on breaking the crockery. Now she is a Christian and has learned to clean the house right through every day quite nicely. She can read in Portuguese, and the other day when I gave her dictation for the first time, she had only two mistakes. Her father is very pleased about her and tells me I am to choose her husband . . . After years of patient training they really do take shape!

13

Not only did Bessie's protégées take shape with patient training, but during that third term, several faith projects also took shape and Bessie was deeply involved in them all. For instance, there was the steady development of the leprosy work. A site of great natural beauty had been obtained near to Bissora for a Settlement-cum-Bible-School and the first buildings had been erected. Throughout the Balanta area clinics for leprosy patients were organised, and although Bessie was not a trained nurse and had a personal dread of the disease, she loved to help whenever she visited. She would give injections or bind up sores, her friendliness helping somewhat to alleviate the suffering. What a day of gladness it was when the first leper converts were baptised.

Michael Tarrant who, as Medical Administrator and later Bible School Principal, worked side by side with Doctor Herbert Billman and a team of nurses, reports:

We used a sand pit full of water. From all the surrounding villages came Balantas, and there was an unexpected group of Cape Verdian traders from Bissora present. First of all Dona H., a grey-haired saint in her fifties, testifies. The crowd surges round the pool as we enter the water. Then one of the greatest thrills! One by one seven lepers come forward, the first-fruits of our leper work in this land. Every one, though pitifully scarred in body, is wonderfully saved by His grace. There is F., the first Christian of the Mandingo tribe in Guinea to be baptised. What a thrill to take his poor mutilated hands in mine and baptise him into the Name. Next comes B., weak, frail, consumed with leprosy and tuberculosis, but triumphant. Following him comes M., a Cape Verdian, recently married to one of our Balanta Christian girls, also a patient. Then comes a little chap, half-white hands and face disfigured by the same disease, but trusting. Then dear J.C.B., more recently saved, a big strong Papel, with such a bright testimony. He loves to go out evangelising with the students. We got him in the early stages of the disease. Then comes our beloved Christian guard and caretaker, the one who hobbled sixty miles to Bissau to be cured and saved. Then comes A., a carpenter. We doubted his experience until recently when the Lord really got hold of him. Seven lepers from six different tribes boldly declared their faith in and consecration to our glorious Lord.

At the same time the training programme for the believers was taking shape in three notable ways—through the 'Fishermen's Classes', through the Bible School and through the newly formed national missionary society under the title of the 'Missionary Alliance of the Evangelical Church of Portuguese Guinea'. The purpose of the classes was to give instruction to those who had a zeal for evangelism, but who, for one reason or another, might not be able to become students at the Bible School. On Monday evenings they went through a Bible message in detail with appropriate illustrations. This was their home-study for the next few days. Then on Friday evenings they were expected to give it back in their own way for comment and criticism before using the talk in the weekend Gospel outreach. This scheme proved immensely worthwhile. Many who got the first taste of evangelism from these classes, went on to be Bible School students, graduating from that to be evangelists, teachers and pastors. They then formed the field staff of the Missionary Alliance whose support was provided, in part at first, by the Church members. It took many more years for this project to be seen in its completeness, but the living seed of hope had been planted and already it was showing signs of vigorous life.

'The Bijagos Islands' was part of the declaration of faith which Leslie had made in Kounkanne back in 1945, while waiting Bessie's return from her memorable visit over the frontier and down to Bissau. He had written down the faith-project, had signed and dated the scrap of paper. Now that part of the vision was to be realised as the first advance into the Archipelago was made. The pioneers were Marie Baaken, Ruth Gardner and a number of the national workers. Together they moved forward in the evangelisation of the Islands. On one occasion while Bessie and Leslie were visiting the workers they were startled by a shout of 'Fire! Fire!' They rushed out to find a hut in flames and several men pulling frantically at the straw roof. As there was a high wind panic soon seized hold of the villagers. The missionaries tried in vain to give some directive to operations. Before long the whole village was a roaring inferno, the flames swallowing one hut after the other. In their distress, some of the villagers poured out palm wine libations, others muttered incantations while others rushed into their idol temples and dragged out their household gods. The missionaries rescued what they could of their belongings, but there was considerable loss. When the damage could be counted it was estimated that more than forty huts and three pagan temples had been burned down.

But we step forward a few more years to read a more recent report by Leslie.

Visit the Bijagos Church and hear them singing the praise of God in their own language. Watch that ex-witch-doctor stand up and give his grateful testimony to the grace and power of God. See this other one proud to follow his Lord in the waters of baptism. At the last conference in the Bijagos Islands, populated by some 10,000 people, there were no less than three born-again ex-sorcerers.

Literature distribution had always been to the forefront of the Brierleys' thinking. It was such a useful tool for evangelism, especially amongst those who thought themselves too well-educated to come to services Right back in the beginning days, Bessie and Dona Libania had visited all round the city of Bissau with Bibles and portions of Scripture. Now in all their travels colony-wide and over the frontiers, Leslie and Bessie never failed to carry a stock of books with them. In most places there was at least someone who could read and who was interested enough to buy. As others were added to the fellowship they too saw the possibilities in this kind of work.

Aristides was one of the first literature missionaries. Starting off from Bissau with a quantity of tracts and a Bible, he walked the miles to Bula, too poor to pay the sum asked for by the lorry drivers. There in the market place he began to witness. Crowds gathered around to listen as with great power in the Holy Spirit he spread the news around. Some mocked at him, but he continued to persuade his listeners and to distribute his tracts until a car drew up beside him and the driver offered him a lift. Taking this to be of the Lord, he got in and was given a trip throughout the whole of that area. He made full use of the occasion for his ministry.

Adolfo and Francisco were others who caught the vision and went out with books. On one occasion Adolfo who had been a dancer with a touring theatrical group, was tempted by the offer of well-paid employment if only he would give up his book-selling fanaticism. But he chose his unpaid task rather than return to his old life. Francisco, out on a selling tour, was given transport by some Roman Catholic priest. At the end of the journey he was asked to pay for his fare by the contents of his case. This he did—and gave them some 200 gospel leaflets.

A book shop, manned by an African brother and appropriately named the Victory Bookshop functioned in the strategic centre of the town. Bessie and Leslie had moved back again into the city into a much larger property not too far from their original well-loved two rooms. This new headquarters housed the missionary personnel on an upper floor, and the book-room was on ground level. It was easy for the passer-by to wander in, browse round the shelves, listen to a gospel record being played or converse with the tall young man in charge.

The suburban Bissau Novo work had progressed with amazing rapidity. Bessie remembered how unwilling and how afraid she had been to move out there. Now there was much outreach in the area, a healthy Church—'the jewel of them all'—had been established and their premises were part of the mission compound. Out there too was the school and the children's work. The number of healthy children under their care increased and so did the responsibility of bringing them up. Every little one brought its personal problems as well as its joys to the 'Garden of Happiness'. Bessie would gladly have stayed put in Bissau Novo, but the city was the place for business transactions, and, as field leaders and administrators, they had to be there.

Many happy memories permeate that upstairs flat of the city Headquarters—missionary romances, wedding dinners, social occasions—and somehow the figure of Bessie presided with dignity at them all.

"Bessie was a queen, a saint but very much in a woman's garb. It was easy for us to confide in her. She gave us many a flashback into her own experiences and her early days in Guinea. Oh the wonder of our God to take a child of the slums, put His fire into her and make her like a queen," wrote one of her colleagues.

Surprise! Surprise! It was the tenth anniversary of their reentry into Portuguese Guinea. Behind the scenes there was a great deal of secret preparation and excitement was running high. Chief-mover was Sr. J.L., a Portuguese businessman. After all, had not the Brierleys stood by him and his fiancée, both of them young converts, when they had decided to get married? Their wedding had been a big event in Bolama for it was the very first evangelical wedding in that city. The engaged couple were well known both amongst the Europeans and the Africans, and the members of her family were Catholic. There had been threats and protests when the wedding arrangements were announced and some of the relatives said they would not attend the ceremony. It had been the talking point of the town and no one quite knew what would happen. The civil wedding at which Bessie and Leslie were witnesses went off quietly. When they arrived, a bit apprehensive, at the Evangelical Church for the religious ceremony, they found the hall packed. Hush pervaded the unorthodox but beautifully arranged church as the simple service proceeded. Afterwards, there were tears of reconciliation and words of apology, for even the most antagonistic had been impressed. Now it was the turn of the Bissau Church under the guidance of Sr. J.L., to return their thanks to God and to their beloved Pastor and Pastora for ten years of unremitting service in the interests of them all. Tastefully printed invitations were sent out. A close friend of Sr. J.L. lent part of his factory building for the celebrations. Not a word was whispered to Bessie or Leslie till all was ready. For a whole evening, the guests listened to a programme put over by members of the Church, dramatising the growth of the work over the years. There were testimonies and choir pieces and even a duet in English. There was a good deal of humour and a great deal of thanksgiving. Finally a presentation was made of a magnificent hand-stitched Madeira tablecloth, large enough to cover Bessie's family dining-table to which so many so often came.

So indeed things did shape up as missionary and national

workers shared vision, prayed together, helped one another, lived for one another's good, pushed out into new areas and used new methods for winning Guinea's sons and daughters to the Kingdom of our Lord Jesus Christ.

An unsolved medical query which gave some cause for alarm and the deep longing to see Norman and Bessie's ageing mother brought them home for furlough at the end of 1955. The news of the first stirrings of revival on the field sent Leslie back in November 1956. Bessie stayed a bit longer in England in order to have Christmas with Norman, now at a time of decision in his education and needing the support of a parent. When, in January 1957, she embarked at London, her friend Theresa went to see her off. Chatting together in Bessie's cabin, they were unaware of the fact that the ship had cast off, and was already out in midstream before the alarm could be raised. Panic, apology, laughter and worry came all together and unbidden, until a river tug was signalled to take the extra 'passenger' off!

Neither Bessie nor Leslie had any thought that the next three years was to be their final term of service in Portuguese Guinea. Towards the end of 1959 however personal and family matters claimed their attention. Bessie's mother, eighty-four years of age and now completely invalided, had been moved to Bermondsey Medical Mission Hospital, where she was receiving the kindliest care, but still was unconverted. It was evident that she would not recover and Bessie ached for her salvation. Norman was in the **Lower Sixth** at Emmanuel Grammar School and making application for a place at a Technical College with a view to studying telecommunications. Thus the Field Staff consented to their leaving on furlough earlier than expected. By then God had raised up a capable missionary force, the Church had passed its infancy and 'walking in the fear of the Lord and in the comfort of the Holy Spirit, it was multiplied'.

That same Church was yet to experience the heat of fierce

persecution, the agonies of a bloody civil war, the loss of Christian leaders in martyrdom, the scattering of believers into hiding places and over frontiers. But so the Church grew and extended until refugee groups became the nuclei of infant Churches in other places.

14

"God has made laughter for me. Who would have said . . .? Yet I have borne a son in old age."

ON THEIR RETURN from Portuguese Guinea the Brierleys had become more than interested in a new development of W.E.C. Another missionary couple, Fred and Lois Chapman, home from West Africa, had launched a literature project which was meeting with a great deal of success. Under the title 'Bientot' (French for 'Soon'), a gospel broadsheet in French was produced for free distribution by direct mail wherever French is the language. Already in its third year, this paper was in ever increasing demand and was having remarkable results in salvation. The whole scheme and setup was attractive. Could not something similar be done for Portuguese-speaking territories? The thought kept disturbing them . . . until they talked it out at Arthur's.

For twenty-eight years the members of Arthur's Mission, Bermondsey, had been in partnership with Bessie. Her picture was on the wall—'Our Own Missionary'—and her work was in their hearts. Some of them had worked overtime to help with her college fees. They had prayed her through and out to the field. They had supported her with regular giving, and had many times given beyond their means in order to provide some special item—an organ, a duplicator, visual-aid equipment, a car and so on. 'Second milers' Bessie would call them, and for such she always had the deepest appreciation and affection.

It is no surprise then to find her with Leslie at Arthur's having tea with the workers and chatting over missionary concerns. They bow together in prayer, and, as they do so the growing conviction that the Holy Spirit is urging them to become personally involved in this new type of Gospel broadsheet ministry is confirmed first to Leslie and then to Bessie. They share their thoughts with the group in the conversation which follows, and those who have been their truest friends over the years see in this another opportunity of active participation in overseas work. Many willing hands will be needed to address, pack and despatch. Many hours will have to be given over to this new task. Already there are volunteers. But this is only the initial step. The call is yet to be tested . . .

The house meeting was at an end. Bessie had given her word of testimony and had ended on the need of the Christless millions throughout the world. She did not yet dare speak a word in public about this further call. The lady of the house, crippled since childhood, felt the gentle nudge of the Spirit. For many years a well-guarded half-sovereign had lain amongst her treasured trinkets. Now she had to do something with it. She had to give it to the speaker. So Bessie left that home with a half-sovereign in her pocket and with the sense that so great a sacrifice must be laid again as an offering at His feet. This gift had to be put towards the new vision, the production of the Portuguese 'Cedo' ('Soon'). The first entry in the official Cedo account book was of that half-sovereign.

The mechanics of such a project had then to be thought through. It became increasingly evident that a visit to Portugal was a must, and for this they would have to know God's timing and His provision if the trip were to accomplish anything. They had been booked to go to Scotland to the W.E.C. Conference Centre at Kilcreggan where a series of week-long conferences were being held during the summer months. It was while they were there that the word of the Lord came to them, giving them His promise that He was ahead of them and making preparations. Then He sealed His promise by His provision.

A middle-aged couple long-time friends of the Crusade were holidaying at Kilcreggan. Mr. F. was not well, suffering from asthma and bronchitis. The summer heat and the crowded meeting hall helped him to decide to stay quietly in his room and read while Mrs. F. went to the evening meeting. Mr. F. picked up a magazine from the lounge table and made himself comfortable in their holiday quarters. As he thumbed through the pages his eye 'happened' on a poem which bit more and more deeply into his soul as he read it.

I planned an ultramodern home,
But a Korean whispered, 'I have no home at all.'
I dreamed of a country place for the pleasure of my children,
But an exiled lad kept saying, 'I have no country.'
I decided on a new cupboard right now,
But a child of China cried out, 'I have no cup.'

The poem went on to highlight the plight of this world's have-nots, until Mr. F. felt ashamed that he had so much.

In the meeting hall Bessie was on the platform, sharing something of their call to literature distribution, a call which was becoming ever more pertinent to them. She explained how these printed periodicals would be like pioneers opening up new areas, how their impact would be felt on the masses of new literates of developing countries and how this medium had world-reaching potential. Her audience was convinced. Returning from the meeting, Mrs. F. paused for a moment at the door of their room and looked at her husband. They both knew intuitively that God had been saying something to each of them.

We lived in an old terrace house, [wrote Mr. F.] with no hot water system, no bath and no inside toilet. When our daughter left home to take up her career we were able to save a little money. With this and a council loan, we planned to modernise the home, to put in a bathroom . . .

As we shared our thoughts that evening, my wife and I, we realised that the time for us to build was not right, and that we ought instead to join in Bessie's and Leslie's vision . . .

Next morning we saw Bessie and Leslie after the service. We testified to God's dealings with us separately, then handed them the money to finance the trip to Portugal . . .

We have since built far better than we could have done then, paid for it and seen God give us far more than ever we could have thought possible.

The visit to Portugal was made in September. God, always as good as His word, had gone before them. One valuable contact led to another till a whole pattern emerged—editor, printer, production team. There was Mrs. Lily Freira who made the introductions and remained involved. There was Sr. José Couto, a printer and Christian businessman, who became editor, and there were others. With their co-operation the first edition of 10,000 copies was launched and mailed to addresses in Brazil, Angola, Mozambique, Portuguese Guinea, Goa, Cape Verde Islands, Macao and St. Tome Island. The planning, the timing, the discussions had all gone so smoothly that there could be no doubts left. This was unequivocally God's doing and it was wonderful.

The title of the broadsheet comes from verse 20 of Revelation, Chapter 22, 'I come *soon*', and the message of the second coming of our Lord Jesus Christ is prominent in every issue. The articles chosen for publication urge the necessity for preparedness for this event, and the printed testimonies selected from a world-wide range of contributors comment on the way of life through faith in Jesus.

As the work snowballed so God added to the number of office staff handling the despatch and answering the hundreds of queries. Work groups were formed throughout Britain to pack and mail the issues for overseas. Missionaries on the field collaborated with the sending bases, and in time the feedback showed that lives were being transformed. The little paper missionaries were pushing their silent way into hospitals, schools, prisons, offices, wherever there were readers who wanted to read!

But in the beginning days 'Cedo' was truly another of Bessie's babies, 'a son in old age', a gift from the Lord to be prayed and wept over, a costly child in terms of hard cash to be found for every issue, a problem child for Bessie who found it much easier to handle people than paper, an infant who filled her hours, for Leslie's abilities were already being channelled in another direction.

His flair for survey work with the production of statistics was being recognised in the Crusade, so that, shortly after their arrival home, he was commissioned to investigate the world situation and to report his findings to an international conference of W.E.C. leaders. The outstanding result of this study of missionary deployment worldwide was the emergence of the '19 Point Programme to Reach the Unreached'. It raised several other matters for consideration—the need for re-examination and re-appraisal of the whole missionary task with particular reference to modern means and methods, the need for detailed survey and printed information, the need for flesh and blood to set up a special survey department to handle the in-come and out-go of information. This is where Leslie fitted exactly into the required dimensions.

"The task is immense, one which throws us back on God, for we don't possess the abilities to undertake it . . ."

By November 1961 the Survey Office was in operation, in the Brierleys' already-tight-fitting flat. The one desk was shared temporarily by Norman and his Dad, both alternating

with their times of study. From there, a series of articles on the
areas of need detailed in the '19 Point Programme' was prepared for publication in the W.E.C. magazine, a monthly
Worldwide Missionary Digest, specially suitable for Bible College students was issued and great stocks of useful information
began to be filed away. Leslie spent hours in libraries reading
and collecting from every available source, making notes on
ethnological, social and religious situations all over the world,
clipping out relevant newspaper articles and passages in
missionary magazines. To Leslie this was life and breath, and
more especially so when his work was to be implemented by on-
the-spot investigations necessitating world tours, long absences
from home and a great deal of organisation and inter-mission
co-operation. All of his training and experience was finding an
outlet of expression. But, to Bessie, whose part it was to pack
his bags, to give her last coin to see him on his way, to spend
hours in prayer and sleepless nights and anxiety, it was the way
of the Cross.

When in 1962 Leslie left for Brazil with visits planned to
West Africa and Indonesia, Bessie's heart was often sick and
lonely.

I can't seem to believe that you are so far away. It all
seems so crazy at times, our lives. I suppose with our make-
up, it couldn't run smoothly like for other folks.

Last night before going to bed, I thought about you on
trek, drinking any old water, and then if you got dysentery
and I not with you. Well, all these things don't bear thinking
about . . .

It is so lonesome without you . . . I miss you so much for
you always made trips more interesting. But there it is . . . it
is so hot here in Switzerland that I can't help wondering how
hot you are too.

You don't know how much I miss you. I just work and
work to stop thinking about it.

'Work and work …' for besides 'Cedo' responsibilities B——— helped in the office of the Leper and Medical Crusade. Then there was Norman studying at college and living at home. There were also overseas students, Portuguese visitors, and missionaries on furlough, all of whom seemed to gravitate to the Brierley flat. Missionary candidates loved the evenings there of open fellowship, young people enjoyed the freedom of the singsong and the opportunity for testimony, while older folk appreciated the relaxed atmosphere and the never-ending cups of tea which Bessie dashed around to provide.

'Work and work …' typing, polishing, visiting, preaching, welcoming, helping, advising and, not least, caring for her mother. The tiring bus journeys to the hospital used up many precious hours. What prayer had gone up on behalf of the old lady. How often Bessie had pleaded with her in word and by letter to come to the Lord. Finally, under the guidance of London City Missionary, Mr. Waller, she did. What a carillon of bells were set a-ringing then—in Bessie's heart, down in Arthur's Mission and up in Heaven!

1963 was Jubilee Year for the Crusade, and Bessie was invited to take part in a commemorative tour of meetings in South Africa and Australia. At first she found it hard to make a decision—who would look after Norman, who would take on her other responsibilities?—until it was pointed out that such visits could be arranged to coincide with Leslie's survey undertakings. This would give her the opportunity of spending some months with him. So she agreed to join him, flying out to Chad, where Leslie met her at Fort Lamy. Together they shared in a conference with the Sudan United Mission leaders before taking a three-day lorry trip to Abéché from where they set out on trek to cover the area proposed for W.E.C. occupation. It was a dry and desert land, and for Bessie, the only answer was cups of tea. But water is scarce. On one occasion at least, she was missed for a while and then triumphantly re-

turned with the needed water, having persuaded some A1
women to let her have it and then to warm it on their fire—and
all this without being able to speak a word of their language!

From Chad they flew to South Africa with an overnight stop
at Brazzaville. When they got off the plane at Johannesburg the
first thing to meet their eyes was a notice on a seat 'For Whites
Only'. The apartheid system struck Bessie so forcibly that it
made her angry. For over two months Bessie and Leslie toured
the Republic, making their Headquarters in Durban, where
Will and Rhodie Dawn were in charge. Will, telling of their car
rides and shared meetings, says:

> There was never a dull moment either while driving in the
> car or in the meetings. Bessie was always the spice added to
> the meat. In all the hundred or so meetings there was always
> something hilarious or tears when Bessie was speaking. She
> would tell of her background and upbringing, her entries into
> Guinea, but, although one could realise it, she never dwelt on
> the cost to herself . . . She relived her experiences, she acted
> her story . . . For a long while we heard of blessings from her
> ministry . . .

And Rhodie adds,
"She had such a spontaneous, happy disposition. She could
make pioneering sound like fun, and *that* was something
different from the usual."

From South Africa, their route took them by the frontiers of
Rhodesia and Mozambique where they met many of their
'Cedo' contacts and other Portuguese-speaking friends. Bessie
had the tremendous joy of visiting Rusitu, the Rees Howells'
mission centre, where she talked with a very old African who
had personally known and worked for Rees Howells. They also
had the opportunity of meeting another missionary who had
served for a term in Senegal. Then they went across Northern
Mozambique and visited the coastal towns for the furtherance

of the 'Cedo' work and the survey. At Lourenço Marques they learned that a man who had been the Acting Governor for a time in Portuguese Guinea was now the Lord Mayor of that city. One day they plucked up courage to go and look him up at the City Hall. He was most warm and treated them with friendship, inviting them to tea. They discovered his home to be right opposite their humble boarding house so one day they walked in through the large iron gates and visited the Lord Mayor of Lourenço Marques. When they sailed for Australia he came to say goodbye at the boatside, bringing with him a pair of shoes which Leslie had left behind at the boarding house! He had gone there to see them but had found them gone, and a very distraught landlady wondering how she could get a pair of shoes to their owner.

For twelve glorious days of water only, Bessie revelled in the luxury of meeting people and chatting to the other lady passengers while Leslie tied himself to his cabin table and typewriter. The boat rolled and heaved and while Bessie enjoyed every moment of it, Leslie endured it unwillingly. They arrived at Perth, then took the train across the Nullarbor Plains and rolled across a wide wasteland for two days expecting every moment to see kangaroos jumping into sight, but not one did they see. One feature of their Australian tour was meeting with Bessie's relations, Bill and Dolly Best. They stayed with them in Melbourne, went picnics with them to the woods, saw the kookaburra and koala in the zoo and had the joy of knowing that their son was to be a missionary in New Guinea. The other memorable feature of their Australian tour was their visit to Brisbane where Gerhard and Audrey Bargen, W.E.C. leaders of the work in Queensland, had organised a youth conference over Christmas at a camp site. Bessie loved every minute of her time with the different groups of young people. Leslie writes:

That conference was strenuous and as usual, although I

had the facts and information, Bessie was the better appreciated speaker. I always knew this of course and have no hesi-
tation in saying it. She conquered hearts with her warmth far
better than I did with my facts. The two went well together I
suppose, but if she was missing it was like having bread and
butter for tea without the jellies and cake. One day when
things eased off a bit we went a walk together for our very
own Christmas treat down to the nearby woods. Horror of
horrors, we were chased off by swarms of stinging mos-
quitoes so strenuously that we never forgot it.

Soon after that, all too soon, came the time of parting again.
Leslie travelled by plane from Sydney over to Indonesia to
continue his survey work. Bessie took a ship for England, with
one thought uppermost in her mind—Norman's twenty-first
birthday was coming up, and she had to be home for that.

It was not long before another invitation came to her, this
time to join a team for the Jubilee Tour of North America.
Again, for a short time Bessie and Leslie were able to be
together. It was the spring of 1964 and Elwin Palmer of North
American W.E.C. recalls the deep impressions Bessie made not
only on the public as a speaker, but on the team as she lived and
travelled with them. Once they had been put up at a hotel, a
most unusual residence for a W.E.C. team. For a day or so they
made the most of all that was offered with a good deal of fun
added in. Then Bessie brought them up sharply. The thought
of what her fellow Crusaders had to put up with, or without, on
the fields made her sick of her own self-indulgence and she said
so in no uncertain terms.

"That was one thing about Bessie," remarked one of her
colleagues, "she was always forthright. She gave it to you
straight from the shoulder."

Her travel in the United States took her over some thousands
of miles and lasted from March till June. It seemed that wherever she went her testimony struck right at people's hearts.

Unpretentious, charitable in all her attitudes, she moved her audiences again and again. She had innumerable invitations to revisit churches and was most popular with the candidates at the Crusade Headquarters in Fort Washington.

Then it was home again, and to a routine which sometimes palled on her energetic spirit. There were, of course, moments and days of great excitement—as when Norman qualified from Technical College, then obtained a position in telecommunications with the B.B.C., and later went to All Nations Bible College. A loving mother watched every move, tried always to be at home when Norman was around, made sure that he lacked for nothing, and just as lovingly let him go when he became engaged to his Janet.

But her absences from London Headquarters' life had unsettled her. She resumed her 'Cedo' ministry, but felt she was not really qualified to sit at an office desk. It irked her much, although she tried bravely to do it to please God. She spoke to Him often enough about her feelings for she knew she could never hide them from Him. She agreed to take some typing lessons too, if that would help. But no, she could not make a go of them either. People were her love, she would tell the Lord. Give her people to whom she could mean something she would often say to Him. What about overseas students, for example? There were thousands of them in the Capital. If only she could find a place large enough to accommodate some of them, a home where they would feel welcome and where there would be understanding. She discussed the project over and over in prayer. She wrote about it to Leslie and felt sure that her longing was about to be realised when a friend who had inherited part of a property offered it to her. But the property had first to be sold so that the proceeds could be divided among the family members. It was hoped that the house could be bought back again but this was not realised. Bessie was shattered, and, for a time she was engulfed in disappointment. But with the thought that surely God must have something better in the future for use as a hostel for overseas students in Central London she looked up again and trusted.

By now the South London Headquarters of the Crusade had come under compulsory purchase order, which required their moving out to Bulstrode, Gerrards Cross, in Buckinghamshire. To Bessie this was an immense trial. To move 'so far away' was just unthinkable! London she loved—"my London", she would say—and a day in the city, when Leslie was away, helped to buck her up tremendously. To window-shop in Oxford Street or to picnic in Hyde Park was relaxation enough.

The move to Bulstrode proved to be not so drastic after all. At first there were endless chores to be done to get the mansion into habitable order. Bessie volunteered for the advance party and set to work with a will clearing and cleaning and cooking for the team of workers. Later, when the staff of all the various departments took up residence and the machinery of a well-organised missionary society was set in motion Bessie found responsibilities in catering for the never-ceasing flow of human traffic and in assisting as hostess—"open hearted, generous and glowing" as one missionary visitor from overseas described her.

Still she wondered if this were the ultimate for her, or had God yet something more precise and more personal for her to do? Was God keeping that house hidden for her till Leslie came back from yet another survey tour? Would they settle after that, he to his report-survey-writing assignment, she to her student care? He was due home soon anyway for Norman and Janet were to be married, and Leslie simply had to find time to be fitted with a new suit for the occasion.

"I'll never let him go away again, never," she confided emphatically and wistfully to her friend. Then for fear of offending her Lord, she added, "at least, never on his own and never for so long."

Leslie did come home in time to get his suit and be at the wedding. What a day that was for Bessie—love and joy and ache churning her all up inside—but, through it all came the glad assurance that her dearly beloved Norman was marrying the girl of God's choice with future service for Him in the Seychelles Islands already planned.

Then, for the first time in years, Leslie bought a car. What miles these two had travelled together along Africa's pot-holed, overgrown dirt roads. And if in those days Leslie managed to hit around 30 miles an hour, Bessie would say in an agitated voice, "Oh Daddy, Daddy!" She was never too relaxed in a car. But this acquisition gave Bessie the feeling that Leslie was at last going to settle, and that feeling made her happy, happier than she had been for years.

15

IT WAS NOT far off midnight when the telephone rang and my husband reached out a hand to unhook it. Moments later I sat up tense in bed as I heard him speak in a subdued voice.

"An accident? . . . Oh . . . oh dear . . . Bessie and who? . . "

The conversation went on for a few minutes. I could hardly wait for him to hang up. He turned to me with anguished face.

"There's been an accident," he said. I nodded. I had gathered that much from the snippets of overheard conversation.

"Bessie has been killed and Leslie is in hospital with severe injuries. Another missionary from Liberia who was travelling with them has been killed too. His wife and young son are in hospital."

The news broke like a great wave over us, knocking us off-balance and crushing us with its weight. We sat silent and stunned, our heads cupped in our hands till the wave had receded and we could share together the details of the news . . .

*　　*　　*

It was the morning of 4th February, 1969. The Brierley flat at Bulstrode was gay with anniversary greetings and birthday cards from the two previous days. Bessie and Leslie had time to

give them only a passing glance as they picked up their suitcases, collected their passengers, Quirino and Maria Baro and
their little son Roberto, and set off in the early morning light on
their way north to Scotland. They were headed for Glasgow
where Bessie was to take part in a conference and Leslie had
lecturing engagements at the Missionary Training College and
the Bible Training Institute. To Bessie it meant a very great
deal that now at last Leslie was having opportunities of sharing
his fund of missionary knowledge and his worldwide vision
with Bible School students. It brought a sense of fulfilment as
much to her as to him. The worthwhileness of all his careful
and detailed study and his long absences away from her and
home was now being proved. He had come to be recognised as a
lecturer of authority on missionary strategem. Bessie was
wifely-proud of Leslie as she sat by him.

They crossed the Border and drew up at Gretna Green in the
empty car-park of the Forge, hoping to find it open. But it was
not. So they sat in the car munching their sandwiches. They
should be into Glasgow by early evening, and they looked forward to the warmth of a welcome from Fran and Elsie Row-
botham whom they had known for many years and had loved
for just as many. For Quirino and Maria it was their first visit
to Scotland. They were on their way home to Cuba from a term
of service in Liberia. Their permits were not yet through, so
they were making this trip really as a time-filler.

The dual carriageway nosed its way through the rolling
sheep-grazing uplands where there are no hedges and few
fences. A slight topping of ice lingered on the side roads, but
the main road was dry. With unexpected suddenness a lorry
was in collision with them. The car was swung right round on
to the other carriageway, strewing pieces of framework across
the road. All but Maria were thrown out on to the roadway.
Bessie who had been in the front passenger seat and Quirino
who had been directly behind her were killed instantly. Roberto
lay unconscious with severe head damage. Maria and Leslie

were badly injured. From the site of the accident, the ambulance took them to Dumfries Royal Infirmary . . .

*   *   *

The night hours ticked by. Sorrow and tears overcame me again and again. I had lost my best friend and sleep was chased far from me—till all at once I was a spectator in a great, hilarious gathering, the kind that Bessie always loved. There was such exuberant, happy chatter, such warm embracing in true Portuguese style, such handshaking. Why, heaven had welcomed Bessie and she was doing the rounds! First there was dearest Mother, then beloved C.T., darling Ernest, faithful Victor with his martyr's crown. There was esteemed Ma Moli, dear sister Win, Formosa, Amelia, Benjamin and a host of others. Joy was full, so full, and there could be no tears. Tears are for down here, and sorrow is self-centred—so I wiped my eyes and bade sorrow go as I understood for a brief moment the joy of heaven. There was beauty and splendour and light. The hush of peace stole over me . . .

*   *   *

When Leslie regained consciousness, Jack Aitken from London W.E.C. Headquarters was at his bedside. Quietly Jack told him of the accident and that Bessie had gone.

As far as I recollect I just nodded and said something like, "Oh yes." It was simply not registering as I was so heavily sedated . . . Afterwards through prayer and reading the Lord gave me a quietness of heart and a new sense of wonder of the Glory to which Bessie had gone. I certainly believe she is far better off enjoying herself immensely, busily serving the Lord in some Martha-like way as well as glorying in her new Mary-like phase. She is in the full glow of reality now, but her work here in the shadows continues to develop. Anything which comes from God has no termination EVER. That is my joy!

125

The funeral service was held on Wednesday, 12th February, at Goldhill Baptist Church, Chalfont St. Peter, near to Bulstrode. It was in this church that Bessie had worshipped on her last earthly Sunday. On that evening the minister, the Rev. James Graham, had taken as his subject, 'The Believer's Death'. Over the supper-table Bessie had remarked to Leslie that Mr. Graham's face had simply shone like an angel's and she thought it was so wonderful. As tributes were paid and thanks were given, and again at the graveside, where fitful gleams of February sunshine patterned the quiet resting-place and the crowd of over two hundred mourners, there was a pervading sense of exultation.

> "Thine be the glory, risen, conqu'ring Son,
> Endless is the victory Thou o'er death hast won."

The notes echoed through the still air as the two bodies were lowered into adjacent graves in Parkside Cemetery some three miles from the Crusade Headquarters.

*   *   *

Greatheart Bessie, gracious in manner, generous in spirit, gentle with motherliness, you lived life to the full, gave to the utmost, loved to the limit. Now you have seen your Lord and those of Guinea's sons and daughters who preceded you to Glory. Your life has made us rich. Your example still inspires.

Up, up all! Give thanks at the memory of such a life.

*   *   *

On February 5th, Mr. Norman Grubb, known as Rubi to all close friends, penned a very personal letter to Leslie from his office at General Headquarters, Fort Washington, U.S.A. Mr. Grubb had been British Secretary for almost all the years that Bessie and Leslie were in Portuguese Guinea. Now he was International Secretary for the Crusade.

My Dear Leslie,

We heard last night that God has taken our beloved Bessie to Himself and that you have been injured . . .

The shock is great. You and Bessie are our own family, and my love for Bessie is such that it is like something torn out of me. But we have our Rock and we stand on it. *Everything* whether it appears good or evil is actually God in perfect love. There is nothing else. Of course we know that precious Bessie is immortally with the Lord and that it is actually 'far better' for her. But we also know that what has happened to bring this about—the accident, the grief and the loss, the present great sufferings and injuries—are also His planned way of love, and we know no second causes. So we thank Him even in this and for this.

I know I needn't say much about Bessie to you, Leslie. We have been too much part of one another all these years for that. They have been years of admiration and thankfulness for her as well as for you, ever since Arthur's Mission days and all the years since . . .

So we know the 'well done' and the example set, the fight well fought and the fruit in her beloved Portuguese Guinea.

I just sorrow with you, Leslie and Norman, and share your sorrows so personally even though our sure knowledge of the love of God in our Lord Jesus Christ overflows the sorrow . . .

Rubi

A TRIBUTE

What do I remember?
The happy laugh
That echoed till a thousand hearts replied,
The tears that chased each other
Down warm cheeks
To feel another's hurt,
The radiancy of spirit glowing from the face
Of one who loved her Lord with uncommon greatness,
The intensity of compassion that moved
Her audience
When the stars shone down through the mango trees
On dark faces held in silence,
Or in the assembly halls of great continents.
These things I remember
And give thanks.

5.2.69   Betty Macindoe